THE HEART BEAT AND THE WORD OF PROPHECY

THE HEART BEAT AND THE WORD OF PROPHECY

Apostles David E. and Marie S. Bumtje

1 Samuel 24:5-6 (KJV)
And it came to pass afterward, that David's heart smote him, because he had cut off Saul's skirt. And he said unto his men, The LORD forbid that I should do this thing unto my master, the LORD's anointed, to stretch forth mine hand against him, seeing he is the anointed of the LORD.

Print information available on the last page.

Rev. date: 05/04/2018

To order additional copies of this book, contact:
Xlibris
1-888-795-4274
www.Xlibris.com
Orders@Xlibris.com
778518

TABLE OF CONTENTS

Prologue

I went to buy a birthday card for my wife's birthday, something quite unusual to me. Coming from a poor background, I never got to celebrate any of my birthdays. Hence, birthday wishes, parties, gifts etc. were all alien to me. Considering all this, when my wife became part of my life, I had difficulty celebrating birthdays with her.

My wife however had been enlightening me on the subject matter (birthdays), and in view of this, I decided to get her a birthday card on one of such occasions of her birthdays. I got to the store called Dollar Tree, and I went straight to the section where birthday cards were stacked. Though, I knew little about buying, giving and receiving cards, so I made up my mind to choose a lovely card for her. I quickly picked the first one, the words on the card were nice, lovely and romantic. As I went through the card, my heart started beating rapidly and I heard clearly, "you can't express yourself in such romantic manner." Immediately, I kept the card back because I was convinced I am not vocally or verbally romantic at the time.

It dawned on me that even if I presented a card with lovely inscriptions, coupled with a thousand dollars to my wife, she would expect something real from me knowing well that I was not into the tradition of giving cards. It would just come to her as fake, appearing as though I desire to imitate the trend of cards giving. She would expect a gift coming from my heart that would be symbolic. Hence, I settled for something my heart would easily agree on.

Introduction

The purpose of God on the earth has always been to establish a perfect relationship with mankind. His ultimate goal is to develop a loving relationship with man. A relationship where He can walk together with man for the benefit of man and the good of the earth.

Back in the Garden, when God created man, they had a specific time of fellowship and we see man hiding from God in one of such occasions because there was the presence of guilt, a witness in his heart which condemned him and drove him from fellowship with the Creator. (Genesis 3:8-10)

Prior to this encounter, God had spoken to man and had given him instructions on what to do and how to live in the garden, so there was already a form of training. Man had already received training from God; man's mind was already programmed in a way to know what God wanted, so when there was a deviation, his heart pricked him and he fled when he heard the voice of the Lord.

God has always sought to lead and guide man in line with His purpose for our creation. He has done this all through the scriptures through different means and He has accomplished this through His word, the Law of Moses, Prophets and Prophecies, His Son, Jesus Christ and His very own Spirit working through the spirit and heart of man.

We live in a generation where men would rather go after signs and wonders instead of allowing themselves to be trained and guided by God and also by His Spirit. Romans 8: 14 say, *"For as many as led by the Spirit of God, they are the sons of God".(KJV)* God has never been concerned about signs and prophecies but in training His children to understand and know His ways so that He can lead us by His Spirit.

The aim of this book is to take us through the training process and the relationships we need to fulfill our call on earth. One word of prophecy, one vision and revelation from God is not enough; if you are sure that you have been called into the ministry, then you most certainly need training to help you fulfill your potentials.

It's my prayer that as you open your heart to receive the instructions contained in this book, God by His Spirit will lead you into a deeper walk with Him and you will fulfill His call in your life in Jesus name.

1

In the Beginning

The account of creation gives us a record of the words God spoke when He created the universe and mankind but the first relationship recorded between God and man in the Bible is that of His voice coming in the cool of the day to have fellowship with man.

And they heard the voice of the LORD God walking in the garden in the cool of the day: Genesis 3:8a (KJV)

From then on, God spoke to His creation directly and in some way the scripture didn't give details. When God spoke to Cain, the Bible didn't record whether he heard a voice or just saw a form, it simply says, *"And the Lord said.",* so from Cain to Abraham, God spoke until He revealed Himself in Genesis 12:7 where He appeared to Abraham. Again, the Bible didn't give us any form but there was an account of the words spoken.

In the early development of Abraham's relationship with God, God's word came to him mostly in visions and utterances but after a while, God appeared to him in a human form in Genesis 18. Note that God had to train Abraham to hear His voice and trust the messages that came through the visions of the night. When Abraham was ready, God came in physical form and Abraham recognized Him.

If you study Genesis 18 carefully, the Bible gives us an account of three men coming to visit Abraham. One of them spoke about the birth of Isaac and the same person later spoke to Abraham about the destruction of Sodom. It was with this third person that Abraham interceded for Sodom. While this third person stayed back and discussed the fate of Sodom with Abraham, the other two who were actually angels went on to the sinful country and destroyed it.

From the conversation recorded in Genesis, we understand that Abraham actually saw God in human form and spoke with Him concerning Sodom. This is God's order; He trains you with little things and then progresses to bigger ones that you can relate with because of your training.

Abraham and his children had different encounter with God and He spoke to them at different times through different means. One time Jacob saw angels ascending and descending from heaven (Genesis 28:12). All the patriarch had was the word of God that came to them through visions and most times verbally as recorded in Genesis 22:11 when God called out to Abraham from heaven.

This is how God guided His chosen until it was time for Israel to be delivered from Egypt. To get Moses' attention, God displayed His power in the burning bush and again spoke out through the fire and gave instructions to Moses. Moses had several encounters with God; he went to the mountain of God severally and in one occasion he saw the Lord's back. God had to hide Moses within the rock so that His goodness will walk through and the mortal will see His back.

After all the experiences Moses had with God, He received the commandments and built the Ark of the Covenant. This was one of Moses' highest achievement, which made way for God's presence in the camp of Israel. But what God placed more emphasis on was His word, the laws and ordinances given to Moses. His word was the guide for them, it was what separated them from other nations.

The Law of Moses was so detailed, it covered every aspect of their lives and how they ought to conduct themselves. It also had provisions for forgiveness through sacrifices and atonement and they were to obey the law completely. Obedience to the law brought prosperity and disobedience brought punishment and death in some cases.

The very God of Abraham, Isaac and Jacob, the God that appeared to Moses left the children of Israel with His law and presence. He didn't leave them without a guide, there were Priests and Levites that read, interpreted and executed

3

the law to God's people. At this time of our ancestral history, the law and ordinances were all that was needed and it was what God guided us with. His written word was what they had and it was enough at the time.

2
The Ministry of the Prophets

God led the Israelites out of bondage through Moses and Joshua brought them into the land of promise. God's word was their guide all through the wilderness but when they conquered the land of promise, they became a nation like every other nation and were faced with different challenges.

At this point in their history, God needed to constantly guide them, give them instructions, rebuke and in some cases encourage them. So, He started first by sending Judges who He filled with His Spirit to lead them through challenging times and deliver them from their enemies. The Judges were mostly mighty men and women anointed for warfare, so there was a need for men who will always speak for God and give the people direction.

Who is a Prophet?

A prophet is someone that is called by God and anointed to speak for Him, one who is filled with the Spirit of God to speak God's mind in any and every situation. The words of the prophets were directly from God, and they had access to God's mind always as long as they were anointed and filled with the Spirit of God.

The order in Israel was for the kings, elders and the people to contact the prophets before embarking on anything because the prophets would speak God's mind and tell the people if they would succeed or fail in their endeavor.

> *(Formerly in Israel, when a man went to inquire of God, he would say, "Come, let us go to the seer"; for he who is called a prophet today was formerly called a seer.) Saul said to his servant, "Well said; come, let us go." So they went to the city where the man of God was living. 1Samuel 9:9-10 (AMP).*

These prophets were not bias and they never prophesied to please the people, whatever they said was God's thought and instruction for the moment.

What is Prophecy?

Prophecy is of two folds:

a. Fore-telling
b. Forth-telling

Fore-Telling: According to the scriptures, to foretell means to tell ahead of time things in the mind of God concerning a person, a family, a nation or even an event, things yet to happen, things that are coming in the future according to the plan and purpose of God.

The Bible contains several examples of this. A very good example for us are prophecies concerning our Lord, Jesus Christ. Moses, David, Isaiah and most of the prophets prophesied about our Savior Jesus Christ and the events that will lead to His birth, death and resurrection.

References:

Moses *foretold the coming of the Messiah: Deuteronomy 18:15 – 22.*

David *foretold the Messiah's vicarious death in details. Psalm 22:1-31.*

Isaiah *and some other prophets foretold the Messiah's birth and the city in which He would be born: Isaiah 7:14, Isaiah 9:6-7. Micah 5:2. Isaiah also foretold very clearly in in details the crucifixion of the Messiah. Isaiah 53.*

Different prophets of old were granted the privilege to see into the mind of God and therefore could foretell His purpose and plan concerning events that would happen years after. So, prophecy is not just any word that pops into your mind or head, it is the word from the Spirit of God, a declaration of God's purpose concerning a person, a church, a nation etc.

Forth-Telling: This means to speak forth, tell out or vocalize what is in the mind of God. It's the declaration of the mind of God or the declaration of a particular word from God to an individual, people, place or event for a particular time.

There are several examples of this but I will like us to consider some. They are very specific and you can almost calculate when they will happen. The first example is the word of God concerning Israel's captivity in Egypt (Genesis 15:13).

God told Abraham that his seed will be in bondage for 400 years and when it was time, the children of Israel cried out to God and He heard them (Exodus 2:23-25). Verse 25 says,

> *"And God looked upon the children of Israel, and God acknowledged them" (Darby).*

This happened because of God's words concerning them, the word of prophecy forth-told had a specific time. In Exodus 3:10, God gave Moses the mission to deliver the Israelites because His word to Abraham was that his seed will be delivered after 400 years.

Another example of this prophecy is in Jeremiah 29:4-10. Note verse 10.

> *For thus saith the LORD, That after seventy years be accomplished at Babylon I will visit you, and*

perform my good word toward you, in causing you to return to this place. (KJV)

The prophet was very specific as to the time the Israelites will be delivered from bondage. The days of Jeremiah were fulfilled and Daniel came into the scene and through the studies of prophecies, he realized that it was time for Israel to return home and he began to pray.

In the first year of his reign I Daniel understood by books the number of the years, whereof the word of the LORD CAME TO JEREMIAH THE PROPHET, THAT HE WOULD ACCOMPLISH SEVENTY YEARS IN THE DESOLATIONS OF JERUSALEM. DANIEL 9:2 (KJV).

All through the Bible, we see these two aspects of prophecies and they are both futuristic words from God, fore-telling is fulfilled at God's discretion while forth-telling is for a definite time.

Prophets in the New Testament

The prophetic office didn't end in the Old Testament; prophecy is an essential part of the New Testament Church and God still leads us today through prophecy but the prophetic now is quite different from what we had in the Old Testament.

In Acts 2:17-18, Apostle Peter confirmed the word of the Lord spoken by Prophet Joel which was fulfilled on the day of Pentecost.

> *And it shall come to pass in the last days, saith God, I will pour out of my Spirit upon all flesh: and your sons and your daughters shall prophesy, and your young men shall see visions, and your old men shall dream dreams: And on my servants and on my handmaidens I will pour out in those days of my Spirit; and they shall prophesy: (KJV).*

The promise was not to anoint or call the sons and daughters into the office of the prophet; prophecy was going to be one of the results of the outpouring of God's Spirit, and that has already been accomplished on the day of Pentecost. Unlike the Old Testament, where one has to be called into the office, we as Christians prophesy, we speak God's word with power because we have been filled with the Spirit of God.

There were several Prophets in the early Church and we still have them in our midst today. We can see this office operational in Acts 13:1-3, Acts 21:10-14. So the office of the prophets is still relevant today but there is also the manifestation of the gift of prophecy.

Prophetic Gift and Office.

The New Testament Church operates in a way that is very different from the Old Testament. By the New Testament, I mean the Church that started on the day of Pentecost. Apostle Paul gave a distinction between the Office of the Prophet and the Gift of Prophecy.

The Gift

But the manifestation of the Spirit is given to each one for the profit of all: for to one is given the word of wisdom through the Spirit, to another the word of knowledge through the same Spirit, to another faith by the same Spirit, to another gifts of healings by the same[a] Spirit, to another the working of miracles, to another prophecy, to another discerning of spirits, to another different kinds of tongues, to another the interpretation of tongues. But one and the same Spirit works all these things, distributing to each one individually as He wills. (1Corinthians 12:7-11). (NKJV).

This Gift of Prophecy like any other gift given by the Spirit of God to anyone He chooses. This gift was operational in the early Church. Here are different instances where this gift was operational: Romans 12:6, 1Corinthians 14:1-40, 1Thessalonians 5:20.

This gift was manifested so much in the Corinthian Church such that a complete chapter of the Bible was dedicated to it. 1Corinthians 14 contains all the lessons we need on this subject.

The Office

And He Himself gave some to be apostles, some prophets, some evangelists, and some pastors and teachers,... Ephesians 4:11.(NKJV)

This is completely different from what is recorded in 1Corinthians 12:10. This is a calling into an office, known as the ministry office. The office of the Prophet is not something you just wake up and start functioning in, you must be called (Hebrews 5:4).

This is not a one-time thing; because you prophesied and it came to pass doesn't mean you are a prophet. There is a clear cut distinction between the gift and the office, so we must be very careful not to assume a responsibility or a call that has not been placed on us. If God has not called you, He will not enable you no matter how much you try or how long you fast and pray.

Most of what we have manifested in the Church today is the Gift of Prophecy because God has given us His word and has filled us with His own Spirit, the Spirit that searches the mind of God (1Cortinthians 2:10-11). The ministry of the prophet is no longer as it used to be, God guides us individually, now we have His Spirit and He has given us Pastors and Shepherds to teach us His word and guide us accordingly.

The Purpose of Prophecy

Prophecy is speaking forth God's word with power but the purpose of prophecy in the New Testament is different from that of the Old Testament. In the Old Testament, the word came forth without fear or favor; it was God's mind at the moment whether it was for blessing, for judgment or whatever, it was blunt. This is not the same with the New Testament.

> *For he who speaks in a tongue does not speak to men but to God, for no one understands him; however, in the spirit he speaks mysterie. But he who prophesies speaks edification and exhortation and comfort to men. 1Corinthians 14:2-3 (NKJV).*

Prophecy in the New Testament is for **Edification**, **Exhortation** and **Comfort**; anything different from these is not prophecy by the New Testament standard. It is very important as a child of God to know the word of God by yourself as this will help you to avoid walking in error, leading others into error or teaching error.

Apostle Paul in 1Corinthians 14:5 did admonish all Christians to prophesy. He was simply asking us to maintain constant fellowship with God so that we can know His mind and thoughts at every given time. But note that he wasn't asking every Christian to become a prophet or to start operating in the office of the prophet. We must be careful how we read God's word; learn to read and study in contest and God's Spirit will open your heart to the truth.

3
The Word of God

God has always given us His word to guide us. We see in Genesis, how the word of God came walking in the Garden, then the word came to Noah to deliver the righteous from the destruction of the world through flood. After Noah, the word came to Abraham and his descendants until it was written in Tablets of Stone and Scrolls.

The word kept coming to the children of Israel, to other countries and kings that were relevant to Israel's destiny through the prophets of old until it was time for the word to be revealed in Human form.

> *In the beginning was the Word, and the Word was with God, and the Word was God. [14] And the Word was made flesh, and dwelt among us, (and we beheld his glory, the glory as of the only begotten of the Father,) full of grace and truth. John 1:1,14.(KJV)*

The very word of God that had come through different means to the children of Israel became flesh and walked in a physical form and He was God in Human flesh, in an earthly suit; His name is Jesus Christ. His ministry was characterize by signs and wonders just like the word that came from the mouth of the prophets. There were several blessings that the children of Israel enjoyed as a result of their obedience to God's word but when Jesus came, He was a walking blessing.

He sent His Word

Then they cry unto the LORD in their trouble, and he saveth them out of their distresses. He sent his word, and healed them, and delivered them from their destructions. Psalm 107:19-20 (KJV).

This has always been God's method of operation; anytime there was trouble in the Land or there was need for deliverance, a new direction, a need for supply, He always sends His word to the rescue. In Egypt, they cried out and God sent His word through Moses. All through their journey to the Promise Land, water, food and meat were provided by the word of God from the mouth of Moses.

God has never done anything without His word. In creation, He spoke and the whole world came into being. The history of Israel is characterized by God's word coming to them at different times and in these last days, His word came in the form of a man.

> *God, who at various times and in various ways spoke in time past to the fathers by the prophets, has in these last days spoken to us by His Son, whom He has appointed heir of all things, through whom also He made the worlds. Hebrews 1:1-2 (NKJV).*

The ministry of Jesus, the word of God was a little different from the word that came from the mouth of the prophets. His words was characterize by signs, wonders, love, mercy, compassion and the best of it was that He came to teach us the principles of the Kingdom of God on earth. Through His death, burial and resurrection, He fulfilled God's utmost desire, which is to put God's word in our spirit. This is made possible by the New Birth.

From creation, all God has sought for is for man to obey His word and live the life that he was made to live. Once Adam fell in the garden, it became impossible for man to live in complete obedience to God, and man's heart was estranged from the word of God but God kept sending His word to man.

When God led the Israelites out of Egypt, Moses was with them and they witnessed mighty signs and wonders done by the word of God spoken by him but they could not obey the simple law given to them so much so that God said, *"... to Moses, "I have seen this people, and indeed it is a stiff-necked people! Exodus 32:9"*

King David was a man that contemplated so much on God's word. He tried all his best to live by the word but he fell severally until he cried out to God in Psalms 51:10, *"Create in me a clean heart, O God, And renew a steadfast spirit within me."*

The only way man was going to be able to live in obedience to God's word would be to create a new and clean heart, a heart that can obey the word of God. The word of God concerning a new heart came through the prophet Ezekiel.

> *Then I will give them one heart, and I will put a new spirit within them, and take the stony heart out of their flesh, and give them a heart of flesh, that they may walk in My statutes and keep My judgments and do them; and they shall be My people, and I will be their God. Ezekiel 11:19-20 (NKJV).*

> *I will give you a new heart and put a new spirit within you; I will take the heart of stone out of your flesh and give you a heart of flesh. I will put My Spirit within you and cause you to walk in My statutes, and you will keep My judgments and do them. Ezekiel 36:26-27(NKJV)*

Your spirit and the Word

The death, burial and resurrection of our Lord Jesus Christ brought about the fulfillment of David's prayers in Psalms 51:10 and Ezekiel's prophecies in the scriptures above. After the resurrection, the new birth became possible because our Savior Jesus resurrected as the FIRST BORN from the death and anyone who would accept salvation will be **born from the death too,** which is to receive a new heart and a new spirit, one that can receive and obey God's word. (Colossians 1:18, Romans 8:29)

When you become born again by accepting the salvation of our Lord Jesus Christ, you receive a new heart with the ability to obey the word of God, the will power to do right and live right. In 2 Corinthians 5:17, Apostle Paul said your old life and nature ceases to exist and all things becomes new. God gives you a heart that can obey His word and like David prayed, you'll receive a *steadfast spirit.* Once this is accomplished, you can now receive and obey God's word at will, unlike the children of Israel, you'll no longer struggle to do right and live right by God's standard.

The new man in Christ, the Christian is a product of the word of God, he is born by the word and hence, living by the word comes natural to him. In 1Peter 1:23 says, *"having been born again, not of corruptible seed but incorruptible, through the word of God which lives and abides forever,..."*

The product of salvation in you is the recreated human spirit, the heart that can receive God's word and live by it. Once you have received salvation, God starts training your spirit by His word. God leads us by His word but our spirit must first know His word, so you must start seeding God's word into your spirit by deliberately studying and meditating on the word of God.

Before you got born again, all the knowledge and information with which you lived and conducted your daily affairs was based on your five senses; your mind was in absolute control of every decision. You received information from your five senses, processed and rationalized them in your mind and acted based on your mental conclusions but once you are born again, that is supposed to stop immediately because the new creation receives information from the word of God and acts by faith.

You will not be able to live the adequate Christian life if you do not have sufficient word-based knowledge; the sole reason why your first point of call after salvation is to go for the word. 1Peter 2:2 says, *"as newborn babes, desire the pure milk of the word, that you may grow thereby,."* You need the word of God first.

Your spirit can only be trained to hear God and live by the principles of the Kingdom through your study of God's word. You must desire to know the word of God the way a new-born will desire breast milk. God's word is the breast milk for your spirit and you must have a good knowledge of it.

King Solomon, the wisest and richest king who ever lived before our Lord Jesus, told us that he acquired wisdom and became the richest man by listening to his father's instructions and teachings.

My son, hear the instruction of your father, And do not forsake the law of your mother; For they will be a graceful ornament on your head, And chains about your neck. Proverbs 1: 8-9 (KJV).

My son, give attention to my words; Incline your ear to my sayings. Do not let them depart from your eyes; Keep them in the midst of your heart; For they are life to those who find them, And health to all their flesh. Proverbs 4:20-22 (NKJV)

His secret was in listening to his father and you can testify that it paid off. The reason for going to Church and attending Bible studies is primarily to study God's word and lay it up in your heart. If you don't have the word of God in you, your spirit will not be a sure guide, and God will not be able to guide you through your spirit if you lack adequate knowledge of His word.

In Proverbs 20:27, the Bible tells us that, *"The spirit of a man is the lamp of the LORD, Searching all the inner depths of his heart."* If your spirit does not know the word of God, how then will it serve as God's candle, God's light to guide you through life? You must go for the word and be skilled in it so that you will be able to distinguish between the voice of your mind and the word from your spirit.

God and His Word: Consistency

One of the major reasons for error caused by lack of training in the body of Christ today is because so many Christians have not been trained with the word of God, they never took the time and pain to study God's word so they are unable to judge prophecies by it. God and His word are inseparable, and there is consistency of God's word from Genesis to Revelation.

The Bible is the revelation of God's word and the complete Body of Truth for the Christian. All through the scripture, you will notice a consistency of revelation from Genesis, and through to Malachi; when God speaks, its follows a pattern even if it's a new revelation, it can be discerned and interpreted by what He said before. His word is always consistent and until you know the scriptures for yourself, you are most likely to misinterpret it.

In today's Church, we have so many doctrines that we continue to wonder if Christ is now divided. This is because most of the people behind the pulpit are not trained and skilled in the doctrines of Christ. If you study Church History, you will discover that what we have as the Bible today was carefully assembled by the Early Church Council.

At a certain point in the history of Christianity, there was a need to separate the scriptures from other writings and God by His Spirit assembled the scriptures that were written in different generations into one Bible. One of the major criteria for selecting the writings that are now part of the Bible was the consistency of revelation, the flow of God's word from one prophet to another. So, if you are called into the ministry or you think you have been called, your first point of call is to study God's word.

When Saul became Paul, he exiled himself from all the teachings and training he had received as a Pharisee so that he could study the scriptures and know God's word for himself (Galatians 1:15-19). He traveled out of Israel but then he returned and stayed in Damascus. This man already had knowledge of the scriptures because he was a doctor of the law but he had to fine-tune that knowledge and rely on God's word for new revelation. Apostle Paul is one man that made so many references to the revelations of God in the Old Testament, and his letters lets us know he had adequate knowledge of the word of God, no wonder he wrote over half of the New Testament.

In one of Paul's missionary journey, he made an outstanding remark of a sect of Jews because of their knowledge of God's word. Acts 17:10-11, is the account of the Jews in Berea. They listened to Paul's teaching but also went home to confirm if what was being preached to them was correct. Just imagine if these Jews didn't have knowledge of the word, they wouldn't have easily believed the word of God preached to them by the Apostle.

This is how we ought to operate as Christians, not just to receive anything because you heard it from a prophet, or because you saw it in a vision or dream. Jesus told the Jews to *"... search the Scriptures, for in them you think you have eternal life; and these are they which testify of Me. (John 5:39)"*. He was simply telling the Jews that the scriptures they read daily contained the prophecy of Him, the Messiah.

Apostle Paul, in his letter to Timothy instructed the young minister to *"Be diligent to present yourself approved to God, a worker who does not need to be ashamed, **rightly dividing the word of truth**. (2Timothy 2:15)"*. The phrase "rightly diving" means to correctly handle, to correctly explain, to rightly handle… These will not be possible if you don't have a huge deposit of the word of God in your heart.

In the same letter to Timothy, 2Timothy 3:16-17, Paul says, *"All Scripture is given by inspiration of God, and is profitable for doctrine, for reproof, for correction, for instruction in righteousness, that the man of God may be complete, thoroughly equipped for every good work."* The scripture is to equip us as Christians, so if you fail to study the word and be equipped, you are in danger of working in error.

The WORD-Advantage

I will like to emphasize here that God's word do come to us through different mediums like dreams, visions, words of prophecies and so on. But you need adequate knowledge of the Bible to judge any word that comes to you. *For God speaketh once, yea twice, yet man perceiveth it not. In a dream, in a vision of the night, when deep sleep falleth upon men, in slumberings upon the bed; Then he openeth the ears of men, and sealeth their instruction (Job 33:14-16).* When our Lord Jesus was tempted by the Devil, He made reference to the Bible to put Satan off instead of fleeing and the devil quoted a scripture to Jesus too. The scripture was very accurate but Jesus knew better, so He rebuked the devil with another word from the Bible. (Luke 4:3-13).

Sometime after the ascension of our Lord Jesus, a certain centurion named Cornelius prayed and God sent His word of salvation to him through Peter. Prior his encounter, the Jews had no dealings with the gentiles, so God had to visit Peter in a vision to convince him to go to the house of a gentile, a non-believer or an infidel as we may put it today. Peter saw a vision and God spoke to him but he argued that he will not eat an unclean animal even in a vision. When he woke up, he was thinking about the dream and the Spirit instructed him to go with the men who Cornelius had sent (Acts 10:9-20).

In verse 19-20, the Bible says, *"While Peter thought about the vision, the Spirit said to him, "Behold, three men are seeking you. Arise therefore, go down and go with them, doubting nothing; for I have sent them."* Peter's encounter is a perfect example of how to judge all things by the word of God. The laws instructed that Israel should not eat any unclean thing and they were also not to have any relationship with the gentles, but God wasn't concerned about food. The vision was to prepare Peter for his journey to the house of Cornelius. With God, the salvation of man, the mission of our Lord Jesus Christ His Son, is more important than the rules and the traditions of men.

Paul, in his letter to the Thessalonica admonished them to test all things and hold fast to that which is good (1Thessalonians 5:21). How do you test all things especially when these doctrines or prophecies are coming from a revered man of God, a senior pastor or maybe through a very convincing revelation-like dream?

John gives very specific instructions in this area. *"Beloved, do not believe every spirit, but test the spirits, whether they are of God; because many false prophets have gone out into the world. By this you know the Spirit of God: Every spirit that confesses that Jesus Christ has come in the flesh is of God, and every spirit that does not confess that Jesus Christ has come in the flesh is not of God. And this is the spirit of the Antichrist, which you have heard was coming, and is now already in the world.(NKJV).*

Here, John instructs the Church not to believe all spirits because of Antichrist which is already in the Church. The fact that the word of prophecy was given by your father in the Lord or the most senior man of God in your church does not qualify it to be from God. Judge all things and all spirits by the word of God. If you don't have the word-Advantage, if you have not been trained or are not being trained in the word of God, if you have not submitted your spirit for training, you are treading on dangerous parts because there is no way to judge prophecies and visions except through the written word of God, The Bible.

In his final admonition to the Ephesian Church in Acts 20:29-30, Apostle Paul said this, *"For I know this, that after my departure savage wolves will come in among you, not sparing the flock. Also from among yourselves men will rise up, speaking perverse things, to draw away the disciples after themselves. He repeated most of these and said some more in his letter to Timothy, 2Timothy 3:1-9. (NKJV).*

The devil will do everything possible to deceive Christians, so we must equip ourselves with adequate knowledge of God's word and sound doctrine, so that we will be able to judge and test all spirits. Do you know that God can give you a word and a senior pastor or prophet will give you a contradictory prophecy that will land you in a mess? It happened before and still happens.

There is a very interesting account in 1Kings 13:6-24; the Lord sent a young prophet to Bethel with specific instructions not to eat or drink anything there. The man went, did his duty and was on his way home when a senior old backslidden prophet ran after him and told a lie of how he had seen an angel. The young prophet believed and disobeyed God's order and it cost him his life.

Never seek man's approval when God gives you His word. The only thing you need to do is to judge your prophecy, vision or word of knowledge with the written word of God.

Once there is a consistency between your revelation and the word of God, then you have your approval. This is the first part, in our next chapter, we will discuss the witness of the Holy Spirit and the Inward witness.

4
The Inward Witness

The training that the word of God gives us is for several purposes like knowing Him, His voice, His ways and His thoughts. *When you submit your heart to the word of God, it will become easy for you to hear and recognize His voice when He speaks irrespective of the means or method of communication.*

In John 10:1-4, our Lord Jesus gave an illustration of the true shepherd and in verses 3 to 4, He explained how the sheep knows the voice of the shepherd and follows when the shepherd calls out. This is as a result of fellowship; the sheep will only recognize the voice of a shepherd that they have been with for a certain period. Our Lord Jesus Christ is our Shepherd and the only way to know His voice is through His word (Bible).

Paul, teaching about the importance of the fivefold ministry offices said this, *"Then we will no longer be little children, tossed and carried about by all kinds of teachings that change like the wind. We will no longer be influenced by people who use cunning and clever strategies to lead us astray. (Ephesians 4:14 GWT)*

This tells us that the devil has employed different strategies to deceive the children of God and one of such is the teaching of false doctrine, so you need to be grounded in the word of God if you don't want to be tossed and carried about by all kinds of teachings that change like the wind.

Once you have the word of God, the next level is the Inward Witness or the Witness of the Spirit. This is actually the first way God leads His children, but you need the word of God to be able to judge the witness of the Spirit because the **Spirit of God only bears witness to the word of God.**

When you get born again, there is really no physical change or evidence of salvation except for the word of God and the Inward Witness which is why Paul said, *"The Spirit Himself bears witness with our spirit that we are children of God. Romans 8:16".* When I got born again, something changed inside of me which I could not explain to anyone. I just knew I was changed and when the devil came against me with accusation, all I had was the word of God and this Inward Witness. From that moment, I knew I was saved, though I didn't look or feel saved at the time but Romans 10:9-10 was the evidence I had against the devil. I could not separate myself from the bible and I could hold it anywhere and everywhere without any concern on how people may look at it. I remember always telling myself that, "I have said the sinner's prayers, I believed in my heart and with my mouth I have confessed the Lordship of Jesus over my life, so I am saved". Then, there was the Inward Witness that though no one could see was very strong and was overshadowed with great joy within me like a man freed from a capital punishment or a deer freed from the hands of a hunter.

God Wants your Mind

When you get born again, your body remains the same, your mind remains the same too and all the knowledge and information you had prior to salvation will still be there but the light of God has already shined in your heart and your conscience which is the voice of your spirit will become alive unto God, and it will begin to act as a guide for you.

The very next thing you need is to start renewing your mind with the word of God, because God needs your mind. You see, before you got saved, your mind was the center of your life because you received information from your five senses into your mind, reason them out and then acted. But after salvation, you need new information from the word of God to replace the old information in your mind. The renewal of the mind simply means replacing all old, fleshly and negative information gathered from the five senses with new information from the word of God.

Teaching on how we ought to renew our mind, Apostle Paul said, *"...that you put off, concerning your former conduct, the old man which grows corrupt according to the deceitful lusts, and be renewed in the spirit of your mind, and that you put on the new man which was created according to God, in true righteousness and holiness (Ephesians 4:22-24." NKJV).* The *old man* here is the man that is ruled and dominated by the five senses and the *new man* he asks us to put on is the Recreated Human Spirit.

In this scripture, the phrases used are *"put off"* and *"put on."* What Paul was actually saying is *"dethrone"* and *"enthrone."* Once you receive salvation, your human spirit that is alive unto God is awoken, so it is time to dethrone the flesh with his mind and enthrone your human spirit with his conscience. This is a deliberate choice you have to make, you choose to allow God's word rule you or remain a slave to your five senses.

Writing to the Roman Christians, Paul instructed them thus, *"And do not be conformed to this world, but be transformed by the renewing of your mind, that you may prove what is that good and acceptable and perfect will of God. Romans 12:2".* The word of God is what you need to renew your mind and if your mind is not renewed, you will not be able to graduate from the good-will, acceptable-will and to the perfect-will of God.

The Mind and the Heart

I will like to explain here that the Mind is the seat of our emotions, the very core of our carnal human nature. For the man that is not born again, his mind can only receive information from the five senses, hence he is carnal and alienated from God. This is the man that Apostle Paul spoke about in Ephesians 2:1-3.

This carnal mind has no connection whatsoever with God but when man receives salvation, his spirit is alive unto God and his mind can start receiving spiritual information from the word of God.

When the Bible speaks of the heart, God is not referring to the organ in your body that pumps blood, but your Inward Man, the man that came alive when you got saved. Apostle Paul calls him the Inward Man (Romans 7:22), the Inner Man (2Corinthians 4:16), the New Man (Ephesians 4:24), and Apostle Peter calls him the Hidden Man of the heart (1Peter 3:4).

This Inward Man, the hidden man of the heart or the heart of man as we may put it is actually your human spirit which became recreated, which came alive the day you got saved. This heart is what received God's word, and once this heart has started receiving God's word and is being trained by it, the mind will then become a slave of the heart (human spirit) and it will become subjected to the word of God.

The prayer of the Holy Spirit through Paul in Ephesians 3:16-19 is for our recreated human spirit. This prayer reveals God's will for us after salvation.

"...that He would grant you, according to the riches of His glory, to be strengthened with might through His Spirit in the inner man, that Christ may dwell in your hearts through faith; that you, being rooted and grounded in love, may be able to comprehend with all the saints what is the width and length and depth and height --- to know the love of Christ which passes knowledge; that you may be filled with all the fullness of God.(Ephesians 3:16-19 NKJV)

Our recreated human spirit is the heart in which Christ dwells by faith. This is the spirit that is able to comprehend God, which knows the love of Christ and is filled with the fullness of God. This prayer will only be accomplished in you through your relationship and fellowship with God through His word and prayers. Once this is done, your mind will comply.

The Candle of the Lord

The spirit of a man is the lamp of the LORD, Searching all the inner depths of his heart. Proverb 20:27

When you subject yourself to the training of the word of God and allow God's word to dwell in you richly, then your human spirit can be a sure guide. This is what God seeks to accomplish in man. He doesn't want us to live from our senses and be carnally minded. Paul gives us a detailed distinction between the man that lives by his sense and the man that lives from his spirit and the danger of living by the five senses in *Romans 8:5-8.*

> *For those who live according to the flesh set their minds on the things of the flesh, but those who live according to the Spirit, the things of the Spirit. For to be carnally minded is death, but to be spiritually minded is life and peace. Because the carnal mind is enmity against God; for it is not subject to the law of God, nor indeed can be. So then, those who are in the flesh cannot please God.*

The man who lives by his five senses cannot please God because the human mind cannot comprehend the word of God. So, we must live from our spirits and make the mind a slave of the spirit, and subject it to God's word. Once this is done, our spirits can be the sure guide.

In the scripture, we see different examples of people who lived from their spirit and were led by the Spirit of God, their reactions to situations were different from that of everyone and the people of their day wondered about their wisdom and excellent character. This is what Job came to understand and he confessed:

> *But there is a spirit in man, And the breath of the Almighty gives him understanding. Job 32:8*

David, Trained by God

There is an interesting account of how God led David through the Inward Witness when He was running from King Saul in 1Samuel 24:1-10.

Now it happened, when Saul had returned from following the Philistines, that it was told him, saying, "Take note! David is in the Wilderness of En Gedi." Then Saul took three thousand chosen men from all Israel, and went to seek David and his men on the Rocks of the Wild Goats. So he came to the sheepfolds by the road, where there was a cave; and Saul went in to attend to his needs. (David and his men were staying in the recesses of the cave.) Then the men of David said to him, "This is the day of which the LORD said to you, 'Behold, I will deliver your enemy into your hand, that you may do to him as it seems good to you.' "And David arose and secretly cut off a corner of Saul's robe. Now it happened afterward that David's heart troubled him because he had cut Saul's robe. And he said to his men, "The LORD forbid that I should do this thing to my master, the LORD's anointed, to stretch out my hand against him, seeing he is the anointed of the LORD." So David restrained his servants with these words, and did not allow them to rise against Saul. And Saul got up from the cave and went on his way. David also arose afterward, went out of the cave, and called out to Saul, saying, "My lord the king!" And when Saul looked behind him, David stooped with his face to the earth, and bowed down. And David said to Saul: "Why do you listen to the words of men who say, 'Indeed David seeks your harm'? Look, this day your eyes have seen that the LORD delivered you today into my hand in the cave, and someone urged me to kill you. But my eye spared you, and I said, 'I will not stretch out my hand against my lord, for he is the LORD's anointed.'(1 Samuel 24:1-10 NKJV).

David was anointed king when he was young, and prior to his anointing, he had been working with God. He wasn't just chosen and anointed by some random act, in fact when Samuel came to the house of Jesse, David was in the field attending to his father's sheep but God was raising him.

King Saul had rebelled against God and was rejected, and so God sent Samuel the prophet to the house of Jesse and said to him, *"...For I have provided Myself a king among his sons." 1Samuel 16:1.* The choice to make David a king was not random. This is made clearer by the events that led to his anointing in 1Samuel 16:4-13.

The very next chapter shows us that the young David had been receiving the training that he needed to be king while he was in the wilderness. He already had a relationship with the God of Israel and was already used to being led from the Inner Man and trusting God. Here is what he said to Saul when he was to go up against Goliath:

And Saul said to David, "You are not able to go against this Philistine to fight with him; for you are a youth, and he a man of war from his youth." But David said to Saul, "Your servant used to keep his father's sheep, and when a lion or a bear came and took a lamb out of the flock, I went out after it and struck it, and delivered the lamb from its mouth; and when it arose against me, I caught it by its beard, and struck and killed it. Your servant has killed both lion and bear; and this uncircumcised Philistine will be like one of them, seeing he has defied the armies of the living God." Moreover David said, "The LORD, who delivered me from the paw of the lion and from the paw of the bear, He will deliver me from the hand of this Philistine." And Saul said to David, "Go, and the LORD be with you!" (1Samuel 17:33-37 NKJV).

Young David could not have known these things by mistake, because he spoke with convictions, convictions that had resulted from his training and fellowship with Jehovah. He already knew God's thoughts and what God wanted for his people even though he was the youngest in the camp, he went out against the giant that the armies where hiding from, not with physical weapons but in the name of the Lord (1Samuel 17:45-46).

There is no way the young boy would have mustered up such courage in a life and death situation if he didn't have a good relationship with the God in whose name he went out for the challenge. **This is what God wants from us. He doesn't**

want us to have a shabby, half hazard relationship with Him. He wants us to know Him in such a way that we will be bold enough to stand for Him and do great and mighty things in His name.

This is why when it was time for David to make the greatest mistake of his life, God's light flamed his heart and restrained him from error. Had it been that he killed Saul in the cave, it would have been the end of his kingship because it wasn't in his place to kill the king. God didn't want David to ascend the throne of Israel by a coup and we praise God that David's heart had already come to know the voice of the Lord.

It was his knowledge of God, his fellowship with God that helped him to hear the nudging of the spirit in his heart when he was faced with a decision to assassinate King Saul. David had gone beyond his own needs, and he was in a place in his life where all that mattered to him was what God wanted. Killing the King would have brought instant freedom to him as we may think but you see God was leading the young man and his spirit had been trained through fellowship to know God's ways.

As a minister of God, your life should be about living for God and pleasing Him. If you are called of God, He will establish your ministry in due season. Christianity is war against the kingdom of darkness, and not about you or your ministry, it's all about what God wants to accomplish with and through you and until you have been trained in the word of God, you will never fulfill that ministry.

Your success in the ministry is not determined by the size of your church but by the purpose of God accomplished through you. The main theme we have emphasized in this book is the word of God, because until you have the word in you, you are not ready for ministry. In Colossian 3:16, Paul said to let the word of Christ dwell in us richly, this is the foundation for a successful Christian life and ministry.

Moses Knew His Ways

When Moses led the Israelites out of the wilderness, the Bible recorded that God "... *made known His ways to Moses, His acts to the children of Israel. Psalms 103:7".* The children of Israel were moved by the signs and wonders they saw Moses perform but he was more concerned about pleasing God and walking according to His law. God unveiled His ways to Moses that is why so many miracles like water from The Rock, Manna from Heaven and Quails were wrought through the hands of Moses.

This is what God wants from His children today. We live in an era of the prophetic where most people seek to prophesy and others run after prophecies. I want to tell you that God is not so much as interested in your Prophetic-Ministry as He is in your Word-Ministry. If you give yourself to the word of God and seek to live by His word, you will understand His ways and end up operating the five-fold ministry offices; you would even become a prophet for yourself because it is through the same inspiration from the same Spirit the written word flows.

God does not want your knowledge of Him to be based on His acts, the miracles and prophecy that will soon be forgotten. He wants you to know Him for who He is and that knowledge can only come to you when you submit totally to His word. The revelation of God that we received by submitting our hearts and minds to His word, the knowledge of Him that we gain will bring about an enduring love for Him that will last forever.

In 1Corinthians 13:8-10, Paul reveals that it is only love that will remain and this love is a result of accurate knowledge because to know God is to love God.

Love never fails. But whether there are prophecies, they will fail; whether there are tongues, they will cease; whether there is knowledge, it will vanish away. For we know in part and we prophecy in part. But when that which is perfect has come, then that which is in part will be done away. (1 Corinthians 13:8-10 NKJV))

Jesus said, *"Heaven and earth will pass away, but My words will by no means pass away. Matthew 24:35".* If everything we know today will pass away and only the word of God will remain, it is wise for us to go for the word because it will not only last forever, it will preserve us in God forever.

The Ministry of the Holy Spirit

The ministry of the Holy Spirit in the life of a Christian and His role in fulfilling our destiny in God cannot be overemphasized. The Holy Spirit is all we need to live successfully here on earth, but I would want to lay more emphasis on something here, the Holy Spirit bears witness to the word of God, hence the importance of God's word.

Before the end of His earthly ministry, our Lord Jesus introduced the Third Person of the Blessed Trinity to His disciples. His name as we know today is the Holy Spirit and He was first introduced in John 14:16-17. Concerning His ministry, Jesus said, *"These things I have spoken to you while being present with you. But the Helper, the Holy Spirit, whom the Father will send in My name, He will teach you all things, and bring to your remembrance all things that I said to you." John 14:25-26*

His ministry is to teach us what our Lord Jesus said and to bring to our remembrance the word of God already stored in our hearts. Here is my question, if the ministry of the Holy Spirit is directly connected to the word of God that you have been taught, what will He work with if you don't have the word in you?

Concerning the consistency of God's word and the Ministry of the Holy Spirit, our Savior Jesus said, *"But when the Helper comes, whom I shall send to you from the Father, the Spirit of truth who proceeds from the Father, He will testify of Me. And you also will bear witness, because you have been with Me from the beginning." John 15:26-27.*

What this means is that we will easily recognize the leading of the Spirit since we have known the word of our Lord Jesus Christ. In other words, we will not recognize the voice of the Spirit if we don't know the words of our Lord Jesus. This is the advantage that David had, he already knew God's ways so when God spoke to him in his heart, he recognized it an acted without doubt.

The Word and the Holy Spirit

I still have many things to say to you, but you cannot bear them now. However, when He, the Spirit of truth, has come, He will guide you into all truth; for He will not speak on His own authority, but whatever He hears He will speak; and He will tell you things to come. He will glorify Me, for He will take of what is Mine and declare it to you. All things that the Father has are Mine. Therefore I said that He will take of Mine and declare it to you. John 16:12-15.

This is the correlation between the Holy Spirit and the word of God. This simply means that no matter how anointed you may think you are, you cannot be led by the Spirit unless you know the word of God and that is why Jesus' ministry first talked about teaching God's word before He introduced the Holy Spirit. If you have not been trained in the school of the word of God, you will most likely make a shipwreck of your calling.

The ministry of the Holy Spirit is to guide us aright by meditating on the word of God. Our Lord Jesus said that the Spirit will emphasize, interpret and bring to our remembrance what is already written in the word. The only way to distinguish a true prophet from a false prophet, a vision from God from one from the devil is through the word of God, because there must be consistency.

So many people are led today by different spirits and when you listen to their teachings and doctrines, you wonder if they know the scriptures. A lot of such people are not even aware that they are being led by false spirits because their foundation is not on the word of God.

The Anointing that Teaches

But you have an anointing from the Holy One, and you know all things. But the anointing which you have received from Him abides in you, and you do not need that anyone teach you; but as the same anointing teaches you concerning all things, and is true, and is not a lie, and just as it has taught you, you will abide in Him. 1John 2:20,27

Apostle John made the above statement because he had come to understand that if you have the word of God and the ministry of the Spirit in your life, you will never be led astray. You wouldn't need any man to teach you because you are already equipped to know and recognize God's voice any day and anytime and you can also judge when it's not God that is talking.

As Christians, we are constantly bombarded by thoughts and information from the world, our minds senses, and the devil etc. so we need the word of God and the ministry of the Holy Spirit to fulfill our calling without reproach.

Once you recognize the call of God in your life, the first step is to avoid swinging right into the ministry. The first and best thing to do is to start studying your Bible, give yourself to the word and the ministry of the Holy Spirit so that your Human Spirit will be trained to become a Sure Guide, a trusted Inner Witness and the Candle of the Lord.

5
Training for Reigning

There is always a training process before one can achieve any given task. You cannot come into your place of inheritance until you have at least acquired the basic skills, knowledge or information that is needed for you to get a head start. God is a wise investor who demands a hundredfold return from all investments, and the good thing is that He first trains you before you start your ministry or whatever it is He has called you to do.

In the parable of talents in Matthew 25:14-30, the master hands over talents, abilities and callings to three of his servants before he sets out on his journey. One of the most important things to note in this parable is that he first gave them talents according to their abilities, and then he gave them enough time for investments so as to make profit. When it was time for accountability, he didn't spare the servant with a single talent.

I want you to observe that he gave talents to three servants and in a particular order of 5, 2 and 1. The master knew their capacity and their level of training, so he gave them that which they could handle. What is important to us here is that they had been trained and the master already knew each servant's capability.

Has God called you into a ministry? The truth is every one of us Christians have been called into one level of ministry or the other. The difference between those making full proof of their ministry and those loafing around or wondering if they have really been called is the level of training they have allowed and received into their spirits. The first servant multiplied his talents from five to ten, the other from two to four; both were hundred percent results based on their talents and capacity.

These three were servants of the same master so they were exposed to the same information, ideologies and methodologies of their master but their talents and results revealed their capacities and the level of training they had allowed and received. God does not like waste so if you are in the ministry, it is high time you straightened yourself out so that you can be relevant to His purpose.

Created for His Purpose

Then He said to them, "The harvest truly is great, but the laborers are few; therefore pray the Lord of

the harvest to send out laborers into His harvest.
Luke 10:2

Once you get born again, you have automatically been thrust into the harvest field and your primary duty is to bring others into salvation. This can be achieved through our involvement in the ministry in different ways. One thing I want us to note here is that the call of God is in your life and it is His desire that you fulfill your ministry without shame or reproach.

Then the word of the LORD came to me, saying:
Before I formed you in the womb I knew you; Before
you were born I sanctified you; I ordained you a
prophet to the nations." Jeremiah 1:4-5

You may not have been anointed from your mother's womb like Jeremiah or filled with the Holy Spirit in the womb like John the Baptist but the truth is that before you were born, God foreknew you. Jesus had you in mind when He instructed the disciples to pray to the God of the harvest to send in more laborers. You must understand that He called you and He is more interested in your success than you could ever be, so do not be in a haste to kick-start that vision in your heart.

Ministry is very interesting and being called a "Man of God" or "Prophet" is something that is fashionable in today's Church and this is one of the reasons for the many failure and errors in the body of Christ. So many people wants to bear these names but they are not aware of the dangers of failing which is one of the main reasons for training. If you know that you have been called by God, do not be in a haste and let Him lead you until your ministry is established. If He has called you, He will definitely take you to your destination. For this, beloved brethren, I can boldly declare the grace God has showed in my life, not being boastful, but able to numerate step by step how God took me from dreams to the full time ministry. (a)Dream: In my heart as a young boy to teen age, I was much interested in three professions: teaching, pastoring and medicine. To cut the long story short, for so long, I always had constant dreams of harvesting these three fruits. Once I became a teacher then a pastor, this dreams turned into one fruit. I would see myself time and again climbing a tree to harvest a fruit, each time I'm about to cash it, I would either wake up or would just miss it. It will look so real that each time I wake up, I would be very disturbed. Once God brought my wife who is a medical professional, this series of dream ended. Then one day the Holy Spirit opened my mind to understand the meaning of these dreams and their fulfillment. (b) Nondenominational: I always have this great love for the children of God regardless of the denomination and I have always yearned for the word of God since as a boy. My maternal-grand mother taught me how to read the bible in Bassa language. I have always spend most of my time with the children of God than with my blood relatives. (c) Apostleship: God connected me from one apostolic congregation to another and I started doing an apostle's work without any idea that I was called to be one even after studies and ordination. It was others who received revelations about the apostle's anointing in my life after I totally surrendered. (c) In deliverance, I was afraid of it even when God delivered a fourteen years deaf and dumb girl in my house, I did not know then that it was a sign from God showing me that this is what he has called I and my wife into. (d) English language: My wife under the power of the Holy Spirit used to help me in the translation from French to English in a foreign land, especially in an English speaking country. One day she traveled to our homeland to visit our orphanage and God expressly canceled the time we agreed on for her return. The time we agreed on was purposely because of her role to translate when I am ministering. On Saturday night, I was in the presence of God wandering with what I was going to do with the preaching engagement on Sunday morning. God knew that I was depending on my wife and He, God, wanted to give me what I needed for His work in the area of language. So, He kept her there for a longer time and she was also worried about the situation, trying to rush to meet me, and God asked her "is it your husband who commands you or Me?" Then God came to me and spoke to me "I am not a respecter of person." That Sunday morning I preached my first sermon in English. Once my wife came back, the brethren told her not to translate for me again and since that time, I started preaching, reading and writing in English with the support of my wife. (e) Marriage: I did not go looking for a wife. It happened on one Sunday afternoon in the midst of church's service under the leadership of a humble woman of God apostle Mercy Bate Tataw. What I had to do when I was asked for my opinion after God has openly spoken was "as long as it is the perfect will of God, yes." Yes, to a lady I had no idea who she was except that she is a pastor just as I am. I was strongly convinced at that second, that second that was to determine the purpose of God in my life, that second to take me to the top of who I was created to be and to do, if I have said no, I would have been the most miserable man on earth still scrambling to know the purpose of my life after missing the ultimate opportunity. We can see this in the life of king David leading to his successful reign. It is all about how God is leading a heart that is surrendered to His leadership. Glory be to the Almighty God who has lavished me with His grace. There was little or nothing I did to be where I am today. I can say this, as apostle Paul did what follow in *Galatians 1:15-16 But when it pleased God, who separated me from my mother's womb, and called me by his grace, To reveal his Son in me, that I might preach him among the heathen; immediately I conferred not with flesh and blood.*

Let me repeat it, it is all about the heart. It is all about the Inward Man. When the Two Tablets of the Law are located in the heart not on the head and the Holy Spirit is leading, surely, smoothly, there is guaranty to find ourselves where He has designed for every single one of His children to be. The problem we have is our own ambition and we turn His vision unto ours and begin to do things by ourselves in His name. There was not power from any man on earth nor from any angel to make a teenager like Joseph a governor in a foreign land, Egypt. Surely if this was told to any human being there were not way to believe. But God Himself, when nobody could even understand the plan, led him step by step to the top. Once you are born again, it is the beginning of the good plan of God in your life; it is the beginning to climb to the top of your mountain whether God gives you the understanding or not. There was only one thing and only one concern in the heart of Joseph: the word of God, and not to sin against God. Even in a land full of idols, surely Joseph could not have been permitted to read the bible even if he had one; he could not even carry one because of the way he left his family. In fact, the Ten Commandment was not yet given and the Holy Bible does not tell us that Abraham wrote any letter except that the word of God was laid in his heart going from mouth to mouth – the word of God was taught to Abraham and as God commanded him, Abraham was to teach his descendant and this was past unto Isaac, then to Jacob who in turn taught his children. This word of God was in Joseph's heart and God was leading him to fulfill the dream nobody knew the explanation nor the way to manifest it. God has a plan for you and all you have to do is to let His word penetrate in your heart, surrender to Him and let Him lead.

Genesis 39:9 (KJV)

There is none greater in this house than I; neither hath he kept back anything from me but thee, because thou art his wife: how then can I do this great wickedness, and sin against God?

Genesis 18:19(NASB)

"For I have chosen him, so that he may command his children and his household after him to keep the way of the LORD by doing righteousness and justice, so that the LORD may bring upon Abraham what He has spoken about him."

Total Surrender

When God calls you or gives you a vision, there is always a gap between the time of the call and the fulfillment of the call. This is the bridge between you and your destiny. This bridge is your place of training and absolute surrender to the Master. You cannot fulfill the call of God without God, so He gives you enough time to get acquainted with Him and be trained in line with your call but you have to surrender to Him totally for training. One morning, God the Holy Spirit spoke to me these few words: "decreasing man is a big issue."

A LESSON FROM SAMUEL, HOPHNI AND PHINEHAS

Eli was one of the last judges that ruled Israel before the kingship was established. He was a man of God, a prophet, priest and a judge. He had two children named Hophni and Phinehas. His children grew up to be Levites and went about their father's ministry among the people without proper training.

1Samuel 2:12-17 gives us an insight into their ministry and the atrocities they committed against God and His children. At that same time, a young boy named Samuel was living in the tabernacle with Eli and he was learning everything about ministry while the children of the priest were busy committing all sorts of atrocities against God. Was Eli aware of their wickedness? Verses 22-25 tell us that he was aware and he even spoke to them, called them to order but it was already too late.

When it was time for the mantle of office to be passed on, God cleared the way for Samuel through the death of Eli and his sons. God means business and He does not tolerate unserious people for too long. The ministry of Samuel ushered in the kingship and he died at a very good age after fulfilling his call.

The problem with Eli's boys is that they were not trained properly for ministry, they grew up and started doing what they saw their father do. But Samuel was in the court learning to distinguish between the voice of God and man, learning to hear from God and learning to minister in the tabernacle. Samuel was entrusted to God but he sure had a role to play in the fulfillment of his ministry as he surrendered himself for training.

There are many Hophnies and Phinehas in the body of Christ today. The fact that your father or mother was into ministry does not qualify you to just step into their office at the event of their demise. Ministry is not hereditary, it is transferred from one person to another. It's an office that operates by strict spiritual principles that can only be taught and learned through submission and absolute surrender.

A LESSON FROM SAUL AND DAVID

The Bible gives us a complete account of the first two kings of Israel and how their ministry ended because of training and ability to receive instruction from the Master which was a manifestation of their capacity to surrender and rely on God at every point in their ministry. The first king of Israel was named Saul. King Saul ascended the throne of Israel in a very unconventional way (1Samuel 9-10).

Prior to his coronation and ascension, there was no physical king in Israel except Jehovah, Saul wasn't from a royal family, he was not raised to be a king, he probably never thought of it but God made him king and gave Samuel the prophet the responsibility of training King Saul. It was Saul's responsibility to surrender to Samuel and receive his training but once his kingship was established, he set the prophet aside and starting doing things his ways.

This is one of the dangers of ministry if you are not trained. It is very easy for the devil to corrupt the good that God has put in you. You must understand that a lie is not necessarily the opposite of the truth but a perversion. God has given you a ministry but if the devil can get you to listen to his little suggestions, before long you will via-off course and start doing your own thing entirely. This was what happened to King Saul.

David on the other hand was raised by God through different tasks and tests. Firstly, he was a shepherd and this taught him to be a provider, a guide, a patient and protective person. After his ordination as a king, he went back to the field to learn some more before God displayed him to Israel in the battle against Goliath. After he defeated Goliath, his next level of training began and he started serving the king as his armor bearer (1Samuel 16:21).

David's training for kingship started first in the field, as a shepherd. Once he had passed that stage, God brought him to the palace to serve under King Saul, so it was time for David to learn about wars and strategies, and also to learn how to be subjected to authority. The degree and level of training is the different between success and failure in ministry. The training David received from King Saul gave him a head start in the ministry and he was the most successful king in Israel, the only king who crowned his own successor.

Looking at Eli, Samuel, Saul and David, you will discover that like Samuel, Eli's successor, David's successor (Solomon) was also very successful; a mighty king who accomplished several feats and has three wonderful books of the Bible to his name. This is because David understood ministerial training and subjected Solomon to such trainings.

Solomon testified of this training in Proverbs when he said, *"When I was my father's son, Tender and the only one in the sight of my mother, He also taught me, and said to me: "Let your heart retain my words; Keep my commands, and live (Proverbs 4:3-4").* For David, training was a big deal and it was very important for him to train his son and thank God Solomon complied.

The Need for Training

I'd like to narrate an event that happened to me before starting ministry. I had received the call but prior to the fulfillment of the call, God delivered a fourteen years girl from dumb and deaf spirit through me in our house church. Just after that, in less than an hour as I entered our bedroom, God spoke to me and said these exact words, "This does not make you a great man of God!"

My heart was already lifted up in pride because the mother of the girl had already taken her to several witchdoctors and many pastors, but I was the one that God used to deliver her. It was not even my senior pastor but I that God used and the event took place in my house. My heart could not wait to take advantage of the opportunity to establish the call but thank God for speaking that day to me.

Once I heard the word of God, my heart dropped like a needle piercing a balloon. From that moment on, I committed my heart to the Holy Spirit to make me a great man of God. I made up my mind not to take advantage of the miracles and the words of prophecy to establish myself as a man of God, or allow people make me a great man of God.

What do you think would have happened to my ministry if God had not intervened? God always seek to demonstrate His power and ability through us but we must be careful not to misjudge such manifestations of the Spirit as God's approval and green light to start a ministry. Thank God He spoke to me at the time of pride and I allowed His Spirit to establish God's work at the accepted time. When this event happen, my disciple maker and other leaders wanted to make me the leader on the deliverance section while I myself needed deliverance; one day they asked me to help in the area of translation when I could not really speak English. I had no idea where all these was coming from; today I understand all that was signs for what was ahead of me. Today, the story is different as God's name is being glorified.

It is very possible that God has given His word of power through you on several occasions and you have seen such prophecies come to pass, people can even start suggesting that you may have a prophetic ministry, as much as this may be true, you need to wait on the Lord, give your heart to His word and His Spirit, then allow Him to train you in the direction of ministry where He wants to use you. In one of our missions in a foreign country, when people began to witness the hand of God through my wife and I, they could not hesitate pressuring us to start a church; a suggestion we rejected until when God spoke and before that, another man invited us only to tell us how he could make arrangement on our behalves to a different country where we may make money. Once we left him without giving him any answer, I told my wife this: "this is from the devil; who told this man that we are looking for money? We will still be in this country and we will never meet this man again until we leave." Few years later, God transferred us to the country this man was talking about after we visited our homeland country. Every single step God has moved my wife and I, He has made unexpected provision and things extremely easy for us.

We live in a generation of signs and wonders and people are easily drawn to such gatherings where there are prophecies, miracles and other such manifestations but I want you to remember that some of these gifts are signs that shows that you are believer. In Mark 16:15-18, Jesus said, *"He who believes and is baptized will be saved; but he who does not believe will be condemned. And these signs will follow those who believe: In My name they will cast out demons; they will speak with new tongues; they will take up serpents; and if they drink anything deadly, it will by no means hurt them; they will lay hands on the sick, and they will recover."*

Miracles and healings are signs that are naturally a part of every believer's daily life but because a lot of Christians don't know the word of God, they run after miracles and healing that they already have. We have Christians going around seeking for miracles, others are looking for one prophet or the other to tell them something from God. Yet, they have the Bible with the Holy Spirit living in their hearts. Do I listen from prophets? Of course yes, I do. Even though my wife and I are also prophets (operating in the fivefold ministries). We do not only listen from others, we even consult some to join us to inquire from God. But, most of the times, once a prophecy is out from another servant of God, my Inward Man receives confirmation or rejection and God gives me discernment.

When God was leading Israel to the Promise Land, the king of Moab by name Balak wanted to place a curse on God's people, and he consulted prophet Balaam who agreed to place a curse on God's people. As the events unfolded, the donkey spoke to the prophet, his eyes were eventually opened and the angel of the Lord spoke to him and rebuked his foolishness (Numbers 22:21-35).

If this were to happen in our generation, some Christians will idolize the donkey, build a temple for it and even go there to wait on the Lord. It is this level of ignorance that the devil has capitalized on. This is why you must wait patiently on the Lord and submit your heart for training, if not, you may just be a pawn in the devil's great deception.

Because of the level of ignorance among Christians today, the business of false prophets with signs and wonders has flourished in our generation. But there is no denying of the fact that we still have the prophetic ministry with signs and wonders, but we have more false prophets who don't know anything about God's word leading several congregations today because most Christians are unlearned in the word of righteousness. Let me briefly mention this here what I have done in one of our others books. First of all, the Holy Bible is the written word of God given to us by inspiration, which means by the Spirit of God (2 Timothy 3:6). As born again, born by the Spirit, once you start digesting the inspired word of God and open your heart unto it to understand, your Inward Man will turn like the foundation of a volcano waiting for any opportunity to react and to be connected. A volcano starts about twenty miles beneath the surface of the earth erupting when it is time. Anytime that a prophecy is given, if it is true but its origin is not from the Spirit of God, your Inward Man would simply reject it. Food is not just food; Daniel saw that it would be defilement eating the royal food. I have attended programs and witnessed false prophets, these diviners blowing the mind of people with great prophecies and revelations but never giving a solution. Because the strategy to grow our congregations and to make money today are prophecies. Because people of God have less times to open their heart for training, looking for easier ways, we are not aware that once you believe the words of these diviners, you believe lies and the devil behind these words would not allow you to study the word of God and you begin to believe in prophecies; instead of the fear of God, even sin would be normal with a superficial Christianity.

David was trained!

I want us to consider the effect of training in the life of Israel's shepherd-king who became the greatest king from whose linage Jesus came. His name is David, the son of Jesse. Take a second to think, was it an error that David and his men happened to meet Saul and his battalion in the wilderness (1Samuel 26)? God divinely arranged the meeting of Saul and his 3000 men with David and his 600 men. Think about it, 3000 trained men against 600 untrained men.

To the spiritual babe (a new born again), it may seem obvious that God gave this opportunity to David to kill Saul, the same man who had haunted his life, despite his innocence. Anyone would jump at such opportunity, especially when such incidence of God delivering our enemies into hands had been foretold already in about 44 verses of the Bible. It is stated clearly in the Bible that God would hand over the enemies of His children into their hands.

When David met Saul and his men, there was nothing and no one that could have stopped him from killing the king because all the guards were asleep but David stated clearly that God forbid him to touch the Lord's anointed. Instead, he chose to take Saul's water jar and spear. Would it be right to conclude that David was ignorant of the ambush that God had strategically set for him to destroy Saul and his men?

David and his men were aware of God's word of prophecy and that such an opportunity where Saul and his men were caught off guard and vulnerable to attacks was a confirmation of prophecy. So, he had the word of Prophecy plus the support and counsel of his men (1Samuel 22:8).

Prior to this time, David had been in constant fellowship with God, remember this was the same young boy who went against Goliath in the name of the Lord, so he had received some serious training through relationship with Jehovah. So when Saul was vulnerable, there was a serious communication and consultation between David, his mind and his spirit.

What did his flesh want?

"Freedom from Saul's pursuit and killing the king will bring about that."

What was his mind, his five senses and his men telling him?

"God has delivered your enemy into your hand this day."

BUT

- It was not God's time, though had He had set the opportunity as prophesied in the 44 scriptures.
- It was not for David to kill Saul.
- It was not David's duty to take Saul out of power.
- It was not time for a coup d'état;
- It was an opportunity for David to learn Patience and God's timing.

- It was an opportunity to prepare a heart that would seek after God and not after fame or power
- God wanted to take away the "I", take away "MY MINISTRY" to give way for God's ministry and call.
- God wanted to take away the mentality and spirit of denomination that obstructs God's will and glorifies man rather than God.

Denomination takes people far from God and far from the relationship with Him. Doctrines are the ways of man and God wanted to take the **"I"** away from David's kingship and ministry.

- David was between the "Words of Prophecy" and the "Condition or the desires of the Perfect heart." That heart that has been trained to hear God, to seek God's will and exalt God in every situation.

True and genuine prophecies are from God but, the process of their manifestation needs maturity and a heart that has been trained by God's Spirit and has been well established on the word of God. It takes God to fulfill the revelations and divine prophecies that has been given to you. I started this chapter by explaining that we were created for God's purpose.

Paul said, *"For we are His workmanship, created in Christ Jesus for good works, which God prepared beforehand that we should walk in them (Ephesians 2:10).* Another translation puts it this way, "we are His handiwork." If you are God's handiwork and your so called ministry is His calling for your life, don't you think it will be wiser for you to let Him train you and establish the ministry in His time?

In his admonition to the Philippian Christians, Paul said this, *"Therefore, my beloved, as you have always obeyed, not as in my presence only, but now much more in my absence, work out your own salvation with fear and trembling; for it is God who works in you both to will and to do for His good pleasure. Philippians 2:12-13"*. He first of all admonished them to constantly obey God's word and he reminded them to carefully work out their salvation because it is God who is at work in us, both to His will and to do His good pleasures.

I will like to establish and explain two important things here.

1. Ministry is not your wish or idea.

You must come to terms with the fact that being in the ministry is not your idea, even if you have desired to go into ministry, the thought was planted in your heart by God so He is the one who is actually at work in your life.

2. Ministry is a part of God's good pleasure.

Thou art worthy, O Lord, to receive glory and honour and power: for thou hast created all things, and for thy pleasure they are and were created (Revelation 4:11).

You are not going into the ministry to express your talents or your knowledge of the scriptures. You are not going into ministry because all your friends are pastors and prophets now or because you are from a family of ministers and everyone expects you to be one too. You are going into ministry because God wants to work out His good pleasures through you. Once you are called, you cease to be your own, and you become God's property in a more serious way. You can only say and do what He pleases. *[19] Then answered Jesus and said unto them, Verily, verily, I say unto you, The Son can do nothing of himself, but what he seeth the Father do: for what things soever he doeth, these also doeth the Son likewise. John 5:19 (KJV).* If most Christians will come to understand the implication and responsibilities attached to the ministry offices, they will beg God not to call them into ministry but the truth is, in our generation today, it is fashionable to be a minister, a prophet, a bishop, an apostle and so on. Some go into ministry after one or two visions that came to pass, after one or two prophecies that came to pass or after they prayed for some sick folks and they got healed. Dearly beloved in Christ, being a minister is the greatest responsibility on earth, so be careful what you wish for and what you intend to go into. *Dear brothers and sisters, not many of you should become teachers in the church, for we who teach will be judged more strictly. James 3:1 (NLT).*

David, after his ordination went through series of tests and one of such tests was for his reverence for the anointing and instituted authority. God gave King Saul into his hands, but he chose to let God establish him as king. There are some spiritual principles that may appear little or as light matters before man but they are the determinants of your spiritual destiny. Without training, you will not know or recognize these things.

A Lesson from Mary

And Mary said, Behold the handmaid of the Lord; be it unto me according to thy word. And the angel departed from her. Luke 1:38.

There is a very serious lesson for us to learn from Mary, the mother of Jesus. She was a devoted Jew whose cousin was married to a priest. This lets us know that she was not from an ordinary family. In addition to this, she was betrothed to a man from the linage of David, as this was a combination of the priestly and kingly linage. This means she probably had a good and adequate knowledge of the word of God.

God sent the angel Gabriel to deliver a special massage to her. This message was one that could have made her haughty and puffed up. Imagine what will happen to you if God were to send His angel to deliver a special message to you. I can relate with what some Christians will do, they will immediately build a temple and establish a ministry of angelic appearance. They are like Jacob who had a dream and called the place the gate of heaven (Genesis 28:11-19).

Mary saw an angel, which was already something big but the angel told her that she would give birth to a child of the Holy Spirit, a child that would be called Son of the

Highest, Son of God, yet she maintained her composure, she remained clothed with sincere humility and in that state confessed, *"Behold the handmaid of the Lord; be it unto me according to thy word" (Luke 1:38).*

This was a statement of humility, Christ-like sincerity and absolute surrender to the will of the Most High God. Remember that the fulfillment of this words were capable of endangering her life because at that time, a virgin could not be pregnant without marriage and she was already betrothed to a man who was yet to have a carnal of her.

When she surrendered to God, He took care of all her troubles. Mary didn't have to go and explain plenty things to Joseph because God had fixed things for her (Matthew 1:18-21). This is exactly what happens when you allow God to establish His good pleasure through you; everything becomes easy and you will realize that the lines will just be falling unto you in pleasant places, the men, materials and resources you need will come at each point.

Understand that no matter how anointed or gifted you may think you are, you can't make God call you or force Him to be a part of your ministry. If He has anointed and called you, you should wait patiently, submit yourself to His word and the training of the Holy Spirit, and serve God under a minister or ministry that is already established until God says, "it's time to go."

6
Relationship, Fellowship
and Communication

The Bible reveals the purpose for the creation of man in Genesis 1:26 where God said, *"Let Us make man in Our image, according to Our likeness"*. This lets us know that man was created with the capacity to have and maintain a perfect relationship with God. This relationship is so important because it is only through such partnership that man can fulfill God's purpose on earth.

The Psalmist tells us that the Earth is the Lord's and the fullness thereof (Psalms 24:1). God is the Owner of the world. He alone knows the original plan for the earth and any man that has ever accomplished anything or wishes to accomplish anything in line with God's plan for earth must have a form of relationship with God.

Here, we are discussing ministry and we have already established that Ministry as a part of God's good pleasure. He called you into the ministry to accomplish a special purpose, to work out His good pleasure through you, so if you must accomplish your duties in the ministry and fulfill His call in your life, you must develop a relationship with Him, a relationship with constant fellowship and communication.

The life of every relationship is hinged on fellowship and communication because through these, the parties involved in the relationship gets to learn and understand one another for their common benefits. In this contest, the parties involved are God and you.

Developing the Relationship

In the Old Testament, relationship with God started through a special visit from Him, a call, message from a prophet etc. but in the New Testament, relationship with God starts in salvation. Once you are born again, God becomes your father and the first and best way to know Him is by studying His word.

The Bible is a mine of wealth, in it you will meet God through His different manifestations and through His walk with His children beginning from Adam to Noah, and down to Abraham etc., this will give you an idea of what you are into. Once you start reading the Bible and studying the word of God with an open spirit, you will begin to discern His voice. From that point, you will learn how to talk to God and hear Him talk back to you in prayers.

Once you understand the act of communicating with God, talking to Him and hearing Him talk back to you, you start learning to live and act in accordance with His leading and His word. This is the most important aspect of your Christian work and this is what you will need for the rest of your life.

God leads us through His word, His Spirit and the Inward Witness. There are several life's situations that are not necessarily in the scriptures from which you won't find any example or how to go about them in the Bible, when such situations shows up, you will need to depend on the leading of God's Spirit, you have to listen to the "still small voice" and "the Inward Witness" for guidance.

Understand that the development of your human spirit is your duty and we have discussed that earlier. When life's situation stirs you in the face, you need to hear from God to know what to do and hearing from Him at such point is a function of your relationship and constant communication with Him. I believe by now that you already know how to hear from God, how to judge prophecy by God's word, you already know the difference between the voice of your mind and the voice of your recreated human spirit. I will like you to know that we always have the advantage because God is always talking and our duty is to listen and hear Him.

Example from Scriptures

ABRAHAM

There are several things we can learn from Abraham who is called the friend of God in James 2:23. This man got an instruction out of nowhere to leave his father's house and kindred to go to a city he didn't know before. The Bible never explained how God spoke to him, it simply says, *"Now the LORD had said to Abram:" (Genesis 12:1).*

There is no detail to let us know if the voice came in a vision, in the noonday, through an angel, a still small voice, an audible voice or if God came in person but the point to note is that Abraham believed and trusted God until he became the father of faith and a friend of God. All these happened because the man had already developed himself to listen, hear and trust God's leading.

MOSES

Moses was another man who had several different encounters and the Bible recorded that God spoke to him as a man would speak to his friend (Exodus 33:11). I would like to point out some uncommon events that happened in the life of this extraordinary man from which we can learn how God leads us. First, was his encounter in the Red Sea. In Exodus 14, Moses had led the children of Israel out of Egypt, and when they came before the Red Sea, God asked him to stretched his hand over the sea and divide it (Exodus 14:14-16).

If you read the full story, you will never see where God spoke to Moses face to face but only by statement, *"And the Lord said"*. Was it an audible voice or how did He speak? If it was audible, the children of Israel would have heard. Remember that there was never an account in the history of man before that time where someone divided a sea but this extraordinary man believed and followed the leading of the Spirit and did what was impossible.

SAMUEL

Samuel was a child born as an answer to the cry of a barren woman who believed that God could change her situation. Hannah prayed to God for a son and pledged the child to God even before she had him. Sometime later, the Bible explained in detail how this young child (Samuel) heard the voice of God calling out to him as Eli would (1Samuel 3:2-15).

Reading from verses 4-10, the scripture implied that it was an audible voice because the boy heard it three consecutive times and ran to Eli to answer. But in verse 15, the Bible again mentioned that it was a vision. How did God really speak to Samuel? Was it with an audible voice and then a vision or was it a vision all together, because verse 10 states that the Lord came and stood? The important lesson for us to learn here is that the boy heard and from then on, God led him by speaking to him. This is the reason Samuel had a great ministry, he was the last judge of Israel and he had the pleasure or ordaining the first two kings for God's people.

DAVID

The story of David is unique because he got filled with the Spirit of God on his ordination and went back to taking care of his father's sheep (1Samuel 16:13). After his ordination, the next thing was that he slayed animals to deliver his sheep and then he killed Goliath which led to him serving under king Saul as one his subjects.

How and when did David learn to hear from God? These details are not recorded in the scriptures but from the record we have, it is obvious that the man had already developed and enjoyed a rich fellowship with Jehovah before killing Goliath. From the death of Goliath till his ascension as king, he made several hard decisions that were constantly in tune with God's will.

How did David know that God would give him victory over Goliath? How did he know that killing king Saul was wrong even after God delivered the king to him in the cave? David was a man that made several mistakes and committed several sins against God but one incident in his life revealed the kind of man he was. He was to bring the Ark into Jerusalem, but as the ceremony progressed, God killed Uzzah (2Samuel 6:1-7).

David's first response was fear, holy reverence and humility. He was afraid of God but he didn't run away from God because he already has an established relationship with the same God. Instead of running, David did something that is very relevant to our lives and ministry. 1Chronicles 13 contains the same story but chapter 15 gives us more details. In 2Samuel 6 and 1Chronicles 13, David carried the Ark on a cart with his generals driving the cart.

In *1 Chronicles 15:2, David said, "No one may carry the ark of God but the Levites, for the LORD has chosen them to carry the ark of God and to minister before Him forever."* How did he get to know this new information? Was this not the same man that used a cart driven by army generals? You see, David went back to study the scriptures and he realized that God had given an instruction on how the Ark should be carried (1Chronicles 15:15).

David's story is a perfect example of how you can avoid mistakes if you have an adequate knowledge of God's word. This was the same man who had killed Goliath, who had led Israel to different battles and won, the same man who would consult God before taking any action (1Samuel 30:8), yet he made a mistake because he didn't study the scriptures to know what God had said concerning the movement of the Ark. Your relationship with God does not replace your study of His word just the same way your study of the word does not replace your constant communion and fellowship with Him.

Walking with God is a complete package. You have to study His word daily, pray and fellowship with Him, listen to His Spirit for guidance and develop your human spirit to be a sure guide (The Candle of the Lord). You will not be successful if any of these is lacking in your life. David was a friend of God, but the friendship did not replace God's order of doing things just the same way your gift of prophecy, vision or healing anointing is not a substitute for your knowledge of His word.

Relationship with God is the only rational explanation for all the great things that are recorded for us in the Holy Scriptures. We also have records of men who have accomplished great things since the resurrection of Christ, men of faith like Smith Wigglesworth, John G Lake, Kenneth Hagin etc. Child of God, you are on the scene now, the only way you can do the impossible for the Kingdom is through fellowship and constant communication with God. So start, it's time to start working on that.

Understanding God's Timing

Have you ever heard the saying, "God's time is the best?" I don't know how the statement came about but I sure do know that it sound like a verse of the scriptures which says, *"He has made everything beautiful in its time" (Ecclesiastes 3:11).* Earlier in this book, we saw how God sent a deliverer to Israel when it was time for them to leave Egypt. We also saw that Daniel started praying when it was time for the captives of Israel to return to Jerusalem.

In God's calendar, there is always a set time for everything because He is the one that orders the season and determines when things should be done. In Psalms 102:13 the Bible says, *"You will arise and have mercy on Zion; For the time to favor her, Yes, the set time, has come."* God is a God of order, He doesn't just do things anyhow. He planned us and planned how He will work out His good pleasure through us, so our duty is to wait on Him until it is time to launch out.

There are several examples of men and women in the scripture who understood God's time. I will like us to consider David first. He was anointed king over Israel when he was a young lad but you see that there was a king already reigning and God needed to train him for the position.

In Galatians 4:1-2, Paul said, *"the heir, as long as he is a child, does not differ at all from a slave, though he is master of all, but is under guardians and stewards until the time appointed by the father"*. There are three important lessons for us to learn here.

1. The heir when he is young is like every other person, he is not different from the servants in his father's house.
2. His father places him under teachers and governors to nurture and raise him.
3. His time of maturity is determined by his father. The scripture above says, *"until the time appointed by the father"*

This is one of the reasons you don't just swing into the ministry because you prophesied, healed someone or performed a miracle. If the Father has called you, your ministry will be established at the time appointed by Him because your first task is to be trained.

David was anointed three times before he eventually ascended the throne of Israel. It was all a part of God's master plan because the king needed training, then some more training so that he will not fail in his duties and destiny. In 1Samuel 16:13, he was ordained by Samuel as king over Israel after God had rejected Saul. Again in 2Samuel 2:4, he was anointed king of Judah and then finally, he was ordained the third time in 2Samuel 5:3 as king over Israel.

As much as several people have explained these three anointing, it was because God was raising the man to be the perfect king through whom the Messiah would come so there was need for a thorough work. What has God called you to do? Do you know the training you require? Do you know when God wants you to start? You can only get to know when you fellowship with Him and meditate constantly on His word.

Abraham is another example of a man whom God gave a promise. God promised him a child but God also needed to work out some things before the arrival of the promised heir and Abraham was not patient enough because he had not understood God's timing at the time of his life. In his attempt to help God, he gave birth to Ishmael whose descendants have become a thorn in the flesh of mankind today.

You should never rush into ministry without the necessary training and guidance from God. If you do, you will make a shipwreck of your faith. Moses was God's appointed deliverer for Israel and at some point in his life, he realized what God had called him to do and he wanted to do it his own way but his actions led him to trouble and he had to run for his life (Exodus 2:11-15).

It took another 40 years for God to craft the deliverer that Israel needed out of Moses before He sent him back to Egypt to become the very deliverer that he craved for that got him into trouble. When Moses eventually returned to Egypt, Pharaoh couldn't do anything to him but obey his command. Your training may not take 40 years but you sure do need God, you need to know His time if you must succeed.

7
Prophets and the Church Today

In the Old Testament times, God's word came through divers means and finally through prophets. There were priests in the temple who interpreted the laws of Moses to the people but from time to time God would raise different men, prophets through whom His words of guidance, deliverance, prosperity and judgment came to different generations.

The era of Old Testaments prophets ended when Jesus was born and in Hebrews 12:1-2, Apostle Paul tells us that there was change in God's order because He decided to speak to us through His Son.

The words and teachings of our Lord Jesus Christ, including His prayers were documented as a guide for us and when He ascended, He again gave gifts to men which included prophecy (Ephesians 4:12). But the gifts recorded in Ephesians are ministry offices to which some people are called. We have all been called to minister by God in different capacities but some people have been specially called and ordained by God just as Aaron and his house were called (Hebrews 5:4).

Again in 1 Corinthians 12:10, we see another gift of prophecy given to men as the Spirit deems fit. This one is not a ministry office. This is where some Christians have missed it. The fact that you prophesy and it came to pass does not mean you have a prophetic anointing and should start a prophetic ministry. If the prophetic ministry is your calling, you will know as you grow in the knowledge of God's word and in His time, He will lead you in that direction.

The purpose of this study is to help us avoid errors and that is why we have placed so much emphasis on the word of God. Any Christian can prophesy and any Christian can have the healing anointing, so how do you know if you have been called? Remember the word, the Holy Spirit and the Inward Witness, if you will give attention to developing yourself in the word of God and fellowship with Him, you will know your calling and the right time to venture.

False Prophets in the Bible

Prophecy is an important subject in the Bible and as such is something that we shouldn't handle lightly because the devil has been deceiving men from the beginning by bringing them false messages. There are several examples of false prophets in the Bible and we have them much more today because we have become more desperate to hear from God and receive miracles.

1kings 22 contains a very serious lesson for us to learn as Christians. Ahab invited Jehoshaphat to join him in a battle against Ramoth Gilead. Before they went out, Jehoshaphat insisted that they will inquire from the Lord. So Ahab gathered his four-hundred prophets and inquired from them and they all gave a green light. Jehoshaphat heard but was not convinced in his spirit, so he asked if there was another prophet; Micaiah was invited and he gave the true prophecy. Have we ever asked ourselves this simple question: "Why were those four hundred prophets not able to persuade king Jehoshaphat, who was not a prophet, in the presence of his host king, Ahab?" The answer is found in his Inner Man; strong fellowship and communication with God and the word of God in his heart. Lies and deceptions cannot convince the Spirit of God in a heart where God is dwelling even if the whole world agrees and seems to be in accord. God in a perfect heart would still say NO. One of the greatest problems we have as Christians is that we seem to be doing what everyone else is doing. Recently, during one of our Sabbath's services, God spoke to us about people being more involved in building mega churches than looking for lost souls. We have begun to act like people of the world. 'A' has to succeed because 'B' has been successful. People often ask, how would I know? The answer is in your Inward Witness. The answer was not in their fruits. There was no way for king Jehoshaphat to distinguish false messengers from right messengers. There was also no indication of having at least one real prophet around. All the prophets available to king Ahab were right there and publicly saying the same thing. Yet, king Jehoshaphat still felt like something was wrong. That's the power of a perfect heart. It's similar to when king David's soldiers saw an opportunity to dethrone king Saul, his heart alone was able to make the difference for the final wise decision. Our generation of believers today is more of the written word of God in the head with empty heart and not fellowship. When the voice of the word of prophecy is louder than the Inner Man, everything is in rush and there is no weight to it. I had an experience whereby after discussing an issue with the man of God I was serving the Lord under, he told me something contrary to what God had told me. I took his advice and God was happy with me. Another time, God asked me to do something that was very emotional to me, and when I discussed it with the man of God, he gave me another advice contrary to what God wanted me to do. As I was walking back and meditating on the issue, the Spirit of God in me was grieved, so I asked God this question "I have always had joy each time I meet my disciple-maker, why is it that I now feel grief in my spirit?" God's answer was "when I tell you to do something, why do you go to consult a man?" I went straight and did what God asked me to do. When you have a trained heart, God can navigate it without confusion nor resistance (John 3:7-8). There is so much confusion and superficiality in our generation because we choose to do things with our head and not our heart. I cannot recall what my wife and I were planning to do when God came to us and asked: "Is it the servant who tells the master what he wants to do or the master who tells the servant what to do?" we simply gave it up. I have been in a program where once I entered the building, God said to me "I did not tell them to organize this program." We are servants waiting on the order from the Master and this can only be done with the heart. God prefers those who wait than those who commit a lot of activities in His name.

King Ahab had neglected God's word over a period of time, so a spirit of falsehood came upon all the prophets in Israel except for one but guess what, he wouldn't listen but thank God Jehoshaphat was delivered that day. This story gives us an example of how you can judge prophecies with the knowledge of God's word.

In his final admonition to the Church at Ephesus in Acts 20:29-30, Paul said false prophets will arise even from within the Church and their main objective is to deceive Christians, cause them to walk in error and ultimately lead them to eternal condemnation. Paul already had encountered one of such false prophets in Acts 13:6 so he warned against them. In his letter to Timothy in 2Timothy 4:1-4, Paul instructed Timothy to preach the word of God because the days of the false prophets are upon us and its only through the word of God that we can judge their prophecies.

One sad part of today's Christianity is that men have drifted away from the original culture of "Waiting and Tarrying" and we want everything now. We do not seek to wait upon the Lord anymore, we are too in a hurry to get it and move on, so the devil has taken advantage of this to establish his dynasty of false prophets and their goal is what Paul said in Acts 20:29-30.

When Christians don't know the word of God, it will be very easy for them to be deceived and that is something that we see every day in this age. Hosea 4:6 tells us the end of anyone who refuses to study and know God's word for himself.

> *My people are destroyed for lack of knowledge. Because you have rejected knowledge, I also will reject you from being priest for Me; Because you have forgotten the law of your God, I also will forget your children. Hosea 4:6*

Your only security from false prophecies and more seriously your only shield from the devil and his falsehood is the word of God. Most of the false prophets today are people who started out as God's children but because they lacked the knowledge of God's word, Satan took advantage of their ignorance and recruited them to lead other Christians astray through falsehood.

8
Some Things to Note about Ministry

We have studied the spiritual and most important part of ministry and in this chapter; I will like us to look at some of the important things you need to know if you want to be successful in ministry, if God has called you into the ministry, if it is His will to work out His good pleasure in you through ministry, the things I will teach in this chapter are some of the things you will need to succeed.

Serving/ Service

a. THE LEADER MUST BE THE SERVANT.

But Jesus called them to Himself and said, "You know that the rulers of the Gentiles lord it over them, and those who are great exercise authority over them. Yet it shall not be so among you; but whoever desires to become great among you, let him be your servant. And whoever desires to be first among you, let him be your slave. Matthew 20:25-27

Leadership in God's house is different from leadership in the world. As a leader in the house of God, as a minister, your duty is to minister to God and His people. It is an office of service that you have been called to serve and not to be served. What most Christians admire and covet in ministry today is the glamor, the honor and the reverence associated with the ministry gifts, they are not acquainted with the service aspect, the praying, intercession, fasting night and day and bearing up the brethren in prayers.

I mentioned earlier that anyone that understands the responsibilities of ministry will pray and beg God not to be called into any ministry office because the work is enormous and there is zero tolerance for failure. *And Moses said to the LORD, "WHY ARE YOU TREATING ME, YOUR SERVANT, SO HARSHLY? HAVE MERCY ON ME! WHAT DID I DO TO DESERVE THE BURDEN OF ALL THESE PEOPLE? Did I give birth to them? Did I bring them into the world? Why did you tell me to carry them in my arms like a mother carries a nursing baby? How can I carry them to the land you swore to give their ancestors? Where am I supposed to get meat for all these people? They keep whining to me, saying, 'Give us meat to eat!' I can't carry all these people by myself! The load is far too heavy! If this is how you intend to treat me, just go ahead and kill me. Do me a favor and spare me this misery!" Numbers 11:11-15 (NLT)*

b. WHO ARE YOU SERVING?

Another important thing to note is that once you are called, God trains you through your service to already established ministers and ministries. There is an order in the Bible I will like us to give attention to. Most people who succeeded their predecessors and did very well in the Bible are those who came into the ministry as servants, those who learned the **"art"** of ministry through service. The time came where I knew I needed a disciple maker after God instructed me to live a congregation, I learned how to fast. It took me one year of which I was praying to God to give me one while waiting, I was fellowshipping in different congregations. Because I had relationship with children of God regardless of the denomination, I was invited one Wednesday to attend bible study. At the end of the teaching, one elder was called to come forth and close the section, once he step up on the podium, I heard in my heart, "that is the man." I left the church that day without looking for him until one day God connected me with him and I began to serve him. A humble man from the Muslim's region with a sacrifice life with heaven as the only goal. Your heart will only connect you with someone with the same heart. Because many servants of God today are ambitious, most children of God are not asking for God to connect them to a person they could serve but instead are looking for someone who can feed their carnal desires. "Prominent" pastors are looking for people they can use to build up a huge resume in order to have the name of bishop or apostle. My wife and I, to the glory of God have served even people younger than us both male and female servants and not only spiritually, we serve the brethren. Serving is a spirit of humility and if you don't have it you cannot fake it. The best is to ask God for it. Many among us are looking to serve for the anointing we covet in someone's life thereby missing the real biblical contest of serving which is humility. The call of God in your life can be higher or lesser than the person you choose to serve. It all depends on God who is calling you. Biblically speaking, it is not because you serve somebody that God automatically is going to transfer the anointing unto you. It was God who chose Joshua not Moses and it was God who chose Elisha not Elijah.

Before Joshua could serve Moses, Moses himself served his father-in-law Jethro, the priest of Midian, for 40 years who gave him his daughter. He shepherded his flocks before returning to Egypt to shepherd God's people. Exodus 3:1-2

Joshua the son of Nun was Moses' servant. He started serving under Moses as his messenger and assistant, through this he was involved in all the major events that happened as God led Israel out of Egypt. He received several trainings including leadership and military training from his boss, Moses who was a general in Pharaoh's army.

When it was time for Moses to choose a general for Israel's army, God said to him, *"...Take Joshua the son of Nun with you, a man in whom is the Spirit, and lay your hand on him; set him before Eleazar the priest and before all the congregation, and inaugurate him in their sight (Numbers*

27:18-19). Joshua had been trained under Moses so God could trust him with so many important duties, and when Moses passed on, he became the leader of Israel There were many prominent leaders and I do believe that never a day had Joshua thought he was the one to lead the nation to the Promise Land, he was just serving and remained a servant. A heart of service in biblical term, is not the one looking for a position or something else than serving. (Deuteronomy 34).

SAMUEL SERVED ELI

Samuel was brought to the temple as a young child to serve under Eli the priest. His mother had promise to give him back to God before he was born, so she fulfilled her promise and brought him to the priest while he was still very young (1Samuel 1:24).

After some years of service, the Bible recorded in 1Samuel 3:19-20 that, *"...Samuel grew, and the LORD was with him and let none of his words fall to the ground. And all Israel from Dan to Beersheba knew that Samuel had been established as a prophet of the LORD.* His prophetic ministry was established by God while he was yet serving Eli.

DAVID SERVED SAUL.

David first came in contact with king Saul when his father sent him to take some supplies to his brothers and others who were soldiers in Saul's army (1Samuel 17:17-18) and in the process he became a champion by killing Goliath. Prior to this, he was already anointed king but his spiritual training had only just begun.

After the defeat of Goliath, he lived with king Saul and served in his army (1Samuel 18:1-5). This was where his journey to the throne of Israel started. Though he was already ordained king, he needed to learn the "art" through service and God trained him in several aspects till he ascended the throne of Israel.

ELISHA SERVED ELIJAH

In 1 kings 18, Elijah the prophet of God stood strong to defend the name of the Lord until fire came down from heaven and in the process he ordered the killing of 400 prophets of Baal and Jezebel, the wife of King Ahab was out to avenge the prophets so he sent a message to the man of God in 1Kings 19:1-3 and the man ran for his life.

As the events unfolded, God told Elijah to anoint Elisha as his successor (1Kings 19:15-16). The important thing I want to point out here is an account in verse 21, "*So Elisha turned back from him, and took a yoke of oxen and slaughtered them and boiled their flesh, using the oxen's equipment, and gave it to the people, and they ate. Then he arose and followed Elijah, and became his servant.*

The Bible didn't record any conversation between Elijah and Elisha before Elijah threw his mantle on the young man but once the young man acknowledged the prophet, he left his father's house and went on to serve the prophet. Elisha served the man of God and when it was time for Elijah to be taken away, the sons of the prophets asked him, *"...Do you know that the LORD will take away your master from over you today?"*...

Elisha was known as the servant who served the man of God Elijah, and when it was time for the prophetic mantle to be passed on, it naturally fell on him. Though it was his destiny to succeed the man of God, he had to receive the office through service. If you have been called by God in any capacity, you will not successfully fulfill your ministry if you have not been trained and this training comes mostly through service as we have seen in the examples above.

Serving under another minister and ministry is the only way you can learn the art of ministry. No matter how anointed you are, you need to serve so that you will understand some other aspects of ministry that is beyond laying on of hands, hearing from God, teaching the word, casting out demons and prophesying, there is more to the ministry so you have to serve. You are serving not because of a position you badly desire; you are not serving because of any reason than the privilege to serve God even though there is a man like you before you.

Administration

a. THE ADMINISTRATIVE PART OF MINISTRY

And God has appointed these in the church: first apostles, second prophets, third teachers, after that miracles, then gifts of healings, helps, administrations, varieties of tongues. 1Corinthians 12:28

The most successful apostle after the resurrection was Paul and one of the reasons is because of his adequate knowledge of God's word plus his excellent administrative skills. One of the major reasons for failure in many ministries today is lack of good or proper administration.

Ministry is not a one man's affair, if God has called you, He definitely will call others to help you and work with you but you need some administrative skills to manage those He will give to you and you also need skills to manage the ministry. This is another reason why you should serve under another minister before going to start your work.

When God called Moses, He told him that Aaron will work with him in fulfilling the ministry (Exodus 4:14-16). While Moses was doing his work as Deliverer and Leader, Aaron was handling the ministry in the sanctuary, attending to sacrifices and oblations. While the two brothers where busy carrying out ministerial duties, Miriam their sister was in charge of some other affairs and she was the first prophetess in Israel. This is a perfect example of administration; everyone knows his or her role and sticks with it.

After this first level of administration was established, the Bible went further to tell us about the Moses and Joshua's relationship. Aaron was a priest, Miriam was a prophetess and Joshua was Moses' aid, servant, helper or minister. Moses went further to consecrate 72 elders from each tribe of Israel to be in charge of some affairs and he gave them some level of authority (Numbers 11:16-30). When Jethro, the priest of Midian and father-in-law of Moses visited him, he saw how Moses was alone under the yoke of work; he called on Moses to order and Moses listened to his advice. Exodus 18:13-26

The Church in the wilderness was well established administratively and that is why it was very easy to coordinate over 6 Million Jews in the desert for 40 years.

David also had a very good administrative structure which was one of the reasons he succeeded as king of Israel. Over in the New Testament, when Jesus started His ministry, several people were following Him but at a point, He selected 12 apostles out of his disciples unto Himself (Luke 6:12-16).

Luke 8:1-3 also reveals to us that Jesus had people who supported His ministry out of their substances. This aspect of ministry is called Partnership today and it is very important to have financial partners if the impact of your ministry will be felt beyond your local community, state or country.

Watch out !

(a)Our Lord Jesus did not choose the twelve in the flesh; it was after a vigil in prayer; after He tarried in the presence of the Father; which means, the Father chose the twelve.

> *Now it came to pass in those days that He went out to the mountain to pray, and continued all night in prayer to God. And when it was day, He called His disciples to Himself; and from them He chose twelve whom He also named apostles:(Luke 6:12-13 NKJV)*

(b)Trust God to touch the hearts of people who believe they are serving God with their substances; not those who think they are giving money to the pastor if you want to avoid intimidation and maintain the sound doctrine.

> *and also some women who had been healed of evil spirits and diseases: Mary, called Magdalene [from the city of Magdala in Galilee], from whom seven demons had come out, and Joanna, the wife of Chuza, Herod's household steward, and Susanna, and many others who were contributing to their support out of their private means... (Luke 8:2-3 AMP)*

b. IMPORTANCE OF ADMINISTRATION

At the morning of Pentecost, over 500 people were filled with the Holy Spirit and before the end of that day, 3,000 people were added and the disciples increased. By Acts 7, the apostles were busy with administrative duties and it was disturbing their ministerial duties so they gathered the disciples and said, *"....It is not desirable that we should leave the word of God and serve tables" (Acts 7:2).*

From then on, they established an administrative structure and it resulted in the spread of the gospel from that day till now. You cannot run a successful ministry without a proper administrative structure and administration is something you can learn from service even if you lack a formal education.

Raising People

There is no complete success without a successor, so it is very important that you train people. Any opportunity to serve is an opportunity for training. So if God has put people under you, you must train them in the word and in ministry.

Earlier in this chapter, we studied about some people who became successful in ministry through service and this could have only been because the people under whom they served gave them opportunities, exposed them to ministry and gave them the training they needed to be successful.

God's good pleasure that He is working through you must be passed to the next generation or else the ministry will collapse and end with you.

And the things that you have heard from me among many witnesses, commit these to faithful men who will be able to teach others also. 2Timothy 2:2

Dealing with Pride and Anger

When God calls you and gives you a big vision, a ministry or a call, it is possible to become proud. Sometimes, when God starts working with you and through you, it is very possible for pride to rise up in you, so you must be very careful not to allow the manifestations of the Spirit in your life get into your head.

Pride can end your ministry before it even starts. Apostle Paul narrated in 2Corinthians 12:7-10 that he had a pain that humbled him constantly because of the abundance of revelation granted to him by God. James in his teachings concerning worldliness in James 4 explains that God resists and elbows the proud (James 4:6).

Anger is another thing that can ruin your ministry. When God called Moses, his mission was to deliver the Hebrews from Egypt and take them to the promise land. Moses delivered them out but never took them in because of anger (Numbers 20:1-13). In ministry, you will come in contact with several people and situations that will test your patience but you must learn to manage your emotions.

You must understand that it is not a sin to be angry especially when people wrong you or ill-treat you. In Ephesian 4:26, Paul admonished us not to sin when we are angry. This will only be possible if you decide to walk away, remain calm and quiet, or ensure you don't make a decision or come to a hasty conclusion when you are angry.

Here is what Apostle James has to say, *"So then, my beloved brethren, let every man be swift to hear, slow to speak, slow to wrath; for the wrath of man does not produce the righteousness of God. (James 1:19-20 ESV)"*. History has shown that words uttered, actions and decisions taken at moments of anger always result in regrets and pain, so put your emotions in check.

9
The Heart Beat or The Perfect Heart

Have you ever heard the statement, "The end justifies the means?" That statement may be true to an extent in some circles but that is definitely not true when it comes to ministry. I defined ministry earlier as God working out His good pleasure in you. He is more concern about the heart with which the work done than the works itself.

Small story

A short life story:

One day, one of our apostles back home was traveling in a bus with a medical student. As the bus was moving, they both stared at the poor people on the streets. So the boy began to boast about how he is going to come back to help these poor people as soon as he is done with his studies. The man of God was amazed to see such compassion for the poor from this young man. Then, God told him to ask the young man this question "if I instruct you now not to go back to school, would you accept it?" Once the man of God asked the young man this question, he reacted harshly and kept on saying "God cannot say that; God cannot say that…" This apostle understood the heart of this young man.

When Saul became king of Israel, Samuel taught him the importance of sacrifices unto God before and after battles. On a certain occasion, God instructed king Saul to destroy the Amalekites completely but instead of obeying God and destroying everything, he brought some animals to offer sacrifices unto God. Here is what the prophet said to him:

…Has the LORD as great delight in burnt offerings and sacrifices, As in obeying the voice of the LORD? Behold, to obey is better than sacrifice, And to heed than the fat of rams. 1Samuel 15:22 (GW)

Samuel explained that God is more interested in our obedience to His word, that is all that matters to Him because He owns all things so there is nothing you can do or give that is not already His but your obedience to Him, living to please Him, living in the light of His word is a choice that only you can make and He wants you to make that choice willingly.

God wants your loyalty, He wants you to serve Him out of love and not because of fame or what you want to benefit but because you love Him. Amaziah was a young king in Israel who did all that was right before the Lord but not with a perfect and loyal heart (2Chronicles 25:2). The man did all the right things but God was after his intent, the motive of his heart, and the rationale behind his actions.

When Samuel went to anoint David as king over Israel, at the sight of Eliab, he stood in excitement thinking the chosen one was standing before him but God said, *"Do not look at his appearance or at his physical stature, because I have refused him. For the LORD does not see as man sees; for man looks at the outward appearance, but the LORD looks at the heart." (1Samuel 16:7)*

Eliab never knew God had considered and rejected him because of his heart. God looks at the heart and it is only a sacrifice from a perfect heart that is acceptable in His sight. With all his accomplishments and conquest, David confessed, *"...You do not desire sacrifice, or else I would give it; You do not delight in burnt offering. The sacrifices of God are a broken spirit, A broken and a contrite heart --- These, O God, You will not despise" (Psalm 51: 16-17).*

Perfecting Your Heart

Man is a creature of ambition, we were created with an innate desire to be great, to do and accomplish great things and as such it is natural to be ambitious but in ministry, you are called to fulfill God's vision and so you need not be ambitious but follow as He leads and let the Holy Spirit be your guide in all that you do.

Ministry is the work of the Lord and it can only be done in God's way. In Hebrews 9:14, the Bible tells us that Jesus offered Himself to God through the Holy Spirit. The only sacrifice that is acceptable to God on earth is that which is offered through the Holy Spirit. God has called you, He wants to work out His good pleasure through you but you must first present your heart to Him and let the Holy Spirit guide you.

If Jesus needed the Holy Spirit to make the offering of Himself acceptable to God, then we need the Holy Spirit more than ever today. The Holy Spirit is here with us today, all you have to do is live by the word of God and ask the Holy Spirit to guide you and make your work and service acceptable to God.

Finally, Paul admonishes us on how to be perfect in God's side. Romans 12:1*"I beseech you therefore, brethren, by the mercies of God, that you present your bodies a living sacrifice, holy, acceptable to God, which is your reasonable service.*

The only way to present yourself as a living sacrifice to God is in the very next verse:

And do not be conformed to this world, but be transformed by the renewing of your mind, that you may prove what is that good and acceptable and perfect will of God. Romans 12:2

Would first of all, as always, like to thank the Lord for His grace over my life.

On a particular day, not so sure what the exact circumstance was, it pleased God to show me my heart. He lifted me up and I was looking at my heart. It was like a deep well, so deep that it was impossible to see the bottom of it. There was light at the entrance of the well, but the deeper I looked, the more darkness enveloped my vision.

Just as the heart that pumps blood in the human body is vital, so is the spiritual heart.

Once, when our car broke down and I went to see a mechanic, he gave me a bill for about $2000. On getting home, I prayed with my wife for God to provide us with the money to pay for the repair. However, something just didn't sit right with me. So, I rang up my neighbor who was into car diagnostics. He went under the car and brought out something he believed was the cause of the car breakdown. I went online to search for the price of this faulty part and I ended up buying a single part that a mobile mechanic fixed for $60. To cut the long story short, we ended up spending less than $500. So, I said to my wife, "You see, mechanics are aware that we know nothing about cars. They are aware that we will not open up the engine when they are gone to confirm what they did and did not do. We trust them and whatever they do. The same way we trust doctors with our health, because we alone cannot do every single thing, so we need to find and trust someone to do the things we can't do.

Only God knows the heart of man and only He can search it thoroughly. When He said in Jeremiah 17:9-10, the heart of man is desperately wicked, as the Creator, He knows what He is talking about. We need a new heart and we need to give this new heart to God and to His word in order to stop it from pumping junk. From the account of the word of God, the first person to get a new heart (or another heart, depending on the version you read) from God was the first king of Israel, king Saul, in 1 Samuel 10:9. However, king Saul refused to give his heart to the word of God. We see here, as already explained, that when the word of God calls the heart, it is all about the Inner Man. king Saul did not undergo a physical surgery to get a new heart. My belief is that even though it wasn't mentioned in the Bible, from the first time man sinned and corrupted his heart, subsequent men mentioned in the Bible who faithfully served the Lord got a new heart from Him and they willingly handed it over to the word of God. Let us go back to the book of 1 Samuel 10:1-10, we can see that when the Spirit of God came upon king Saul, he prophesied, but only after the Spirit of God came upon him, and signs were performed. We see the difference between prophesying, signs and wonders, and the importance of a new heart. Signs and wonders and prophecies are from the Spirit of God, but a heart of man is under man's responsibility. God expects our services to come from our hearts because God and man will come together for fellowship. Prophecies, signs and wonders are gifts from God and can stop even while man lives. However, the heart of man will keep breathing as long as he lives. Therefore, the responsibility of maintaining the heart lies solely on man. Just like it is our responsibility to service our cars, it is God's responsibility to give us a new heart just as it is the responsibility of car manufacturers to manufacture new parts for their vehicle, but it is not their responsibility to maintain the car once it is sold out. The more a new heart is maintained, the more fellowship and good things will flow from such heart. There are times when my wife and I were naturally doing the things of God, only for God to confirm at the end that He had been leading us all along.

God has never surprised man. He leads us like we are newborns. It is quite disturbing to me when I see children of God trying to separate the Old Testament from the New Testament. In regard to the heart, we can see how the Old Testament — the first church and the era of Moses — is the blueprint of the New Testament church. It is not the church alone, but also God's creation from the beginning, step by step, gradually and progressively like an architect: the first day, the first man, etc. When the nation of Israel became a free nation, a consecrated nation, and a holy nation, God decided to come down and dwell in the midst of His people. According to studies, the tabernacle or the tent of meeting or sanctuary was erected a year after the Passover (when the Israelites were freed from slavery) Exodus 25:8. Before then, the heart of man was still and deformed with the old heart serving idols. We can see this in Genesis 35:1 when God visited Jacob and he asked his children to bring out and bury the household gods. God knew that the old heart was still in need of a visual and physical presence of Him in order to believe. More so, if you take Egypt as an example, a country with four hundred years of serving idols and Pharaoh as god, it would have being catastrophic for God to appear and instruct them to forget about the four hundred years in the midst of idols and believe in Him when even Moses with the Burning Bush had hard time to believe God and so, could not believe able to make people believe in God without a consistent God's tangible and visible presence different from the ones in Egypt they used too. So, the building of the tabernacle. He appeared as a pillar of cloud by day and a pillar of fire by night. We can again see with Moses the steps of dealing with an old heart that has been attached to idols and physical presence of a god. He went up to Mount Sinai for 40 days without giving any feedback to his people. Since no one had seen or heard from him, they gathered their gold to form a golden calf that they worshipped in place of God — their habit of worshiping a visually tangible gods. God knew what their heart had been used to for ten generations. The word of God tells us two things about this period leading to the period of a new heart: 1- *[29] And since this is true, we shouldn't think of God as an idol designed by craftsmen from gold or silver or stone. [30] "God overlooked people's ignorance about these things in earlier times, but now he commands everyone everywhere to repent of their sins and turn to him Acts 17:29-30(NLT). 2- [23] But before faith came, we were kept under guard by the law, kept for the faith which would afterward be revealed. [24] Therefore the law was our tutor to bring us to Christ, that we might be justified by faith. Galatians 3:23-24 (NKJV).* We can now understand the events of that time from the visual to the spiritual—from seen to unseen. Until man was given a new heart, he was asked to have faith in the unseen. Again, God did not just land man into faith, it was done one step at a time and it was done thoroughly. In each step, God knew what was necessary for every man to fellowship with Him, and He provided it. God did not ask anything else from man but to surrender his heart—the new heart that is given to him— back to God The most important thing that was in the Ark of God was the Two Stone Tablets (the word of God) following 1 kings 8:9. We mentioned earlier about how the Spirit of God came upon king Saul and how he prophesied. God gave him a new heart, but only after he had heard the word of God from Samuel. We continue to understand how the word of God and His Spirit are inseparable. Once the word of God has been deposited into a perfect heart, the manifestation of the Spirit is evident and visible. In Acts 10, Cornelius and his household heard the word of God from Apostle Peter before the Holy Spirit came upon them. Cornelius's good deeds were not able to lead him to receive the gift of speaking new languages. He needed to hear the word of God about our Savior Jesus Christ before he could receive a new heart and then the baptism of the Holy Spirit. According to 1 Corinthians 6:15-20, our body is the temple of the Holy Spirit. But our heart carries the Ark of God where the Two Stone Tablets are located. The more the word of God is in our heart, the more we are able to live by His word, and the more we will be in fellowship with Him. I remember when I was a lot younger than I am now, was evangelizing on the streets one afternoon. I met a man who was older than I was back then. So, I stopped him to share the Good News. When I realized he was a believer, I requested that he permit me to go look for those who are still out there. He protested and said to me "some people are closer to God than others." That statement has remained with me till this day. It is a true and biblical statement, but it all depends on how everyone of us who are called His, who has received a new heart, and surrenders it to God. Those who desire more fellowship with Him are different from those who desire the fellowship and at the same time the care of this life. If you surrender 50%, you will receive 50% fellowship and the remaining 50% will be under your care (struggles); if you surrender 100%, you will receive 100% fellowship and 0% struggles. For years, I have disciplined myself to study the word of God and to read the entire Holy Bible once a year. My heart and my mind have to breathe and pump the word of God.

Psalm 19:7-13

The law of the LORD is perfect, converting the soul: the testimony of the LORD is sure, making wise the simple. The statutes of the LORD are right, rejoicing the heart: the commandment of the LORD is pure, enlightening the eyes.⁹ The fear of the LORD is clean, enduring for ever: the judgments of the LORD are true and righteous altogether. More to be desired are they than gold, yea, than much fine gold: sweeter also than honey and the honeycomb. Moreover by them is thy servant warned: and in keeping of them there is great reward. Who can understand his errors? cleanse thou me from secret faults Keep back thy servant also from presumptuous sins; let them not have dominion over me: then shall I be upright, and I shall be innocent from the great transgression.

I believe that I have been able to show from the Scriptures the supremacy of the word of God and all that you need for a successful ministry. If you will prayerfully study and apply all the instructions and teachings so far, you will fulfill the call of God in your life and still have a great reward in heaven.

God bless you.

Books From The Same Authors:

1. The Original Plan of God For Marriage
2. Personal Deliverance Ministry
3. The Road to Heaven
4. Understanding the Mystery & Power of a Living Faith
5. The School of Life For the Followers of Jesus Christ. Part v. The School of Prayer
6. The School of Life For the Followers of Jesus Christ. Parts 1,2,3&4 – Life on earth planet – The School of Contentment – The School of Worries – The School of Forgiveness.